Jane Edwards

London Interiors
Intérieurs de Londres

Edited by | Sous la direction de | Herausgegeben von

Angelika Taschen

TASCHEN

KÖLN MADRID LONDON NEW YORK PARIS TOKYO

Endpapers | Pages de garde | Vorsatzpapier:
The Thames, Houses of Parliament and Big Ben seen from the London Eye, London SE1
La Tamise, le Parlement et Big Ben vus du London Eye, Londres SE1
Blick vom »London Eye« auf die Themse, das Parlament und Big Ben, London SE1
Photo: Julian Anderson

Page 2/3 | Page 2/3 | Seite 2/3:
Notting Hill, London W11
Photo: Julian Anderson

Page 7 | Page 7 | Seite 7:
Outer Circle, Regent's Park, London NW1
Photo: Julian Anderson

© 2000 Benedikt Taschen Verlag GmbH
Hohenzollernring 53, D–50672 Köln
www.taschen.com

Edited and layout by Angelika Taschen, Cologne
Texts edited by Ursula Fethke, Cologne
Production by Ute Wachendorf, Cologne
German translation by Gabriele-Sabine Gugetzer, Hamburg
French translation by Philippe Safavi, Paris

Printed in Austria

ISBN 3–8228–6218–5 (English/German cover)
ISBN 3–8228–6155–3 (French cover)

Contents
Sommaire
Inhalt

All black and white photos by Julian Anderson
Photographies noir et blanc de Julian Anderson
Alle Schwarzweißfotos von Julian Anderson

Outer Circle, London NW1

Kaleidoscopic London
By Jane Edwards

Le kaléidoscope londonien
De Jane Edwards

Kaleidoskop London
Von Jane Edwards

Arundel Gardens, London W11

London has always been a remarkably compelling city, but as we begin the new millennium it has an especially magnetic hold on our imagination. Its attractions are as many and diverse as the city itself, but it also has the reputation of being an unfriendly place, an insider's city inhabited by disdainful and arrogant Londoners. But also it is arguable that the infamous London aloofness is one of the city's attractions, especially for anyone drawn to its reputation as a fermenting ground for art, fashion and music. Cracking London has to be the ultimate creative challenge.

Today sees London is riding a wave of economic optimism and resurgent creativity, but historically it has always been a city in a state of perpetual change and regeneration. Over 2,000 years it has grown out from the banks of the River Thames to become the sprawling metropolis it now is, dominating the South-East of England. There was never a grand planning vision, unlike Paris or Rome. Instead it has evolved organically, with waves of sporadic property development dictated by the ebbs and flows in the economy. The city started life as a centre of trade and finance and continues to be one. This constant regeneration has created an ever-changing landscape. The modernising Victorians were particularly keen to get rid of old churches and buildings in the name of progress. The result is either a vibrant city of unexpected contrasts, or a disparate hotchpotch of architectural styles, depending on your point of view. But a wonderful side effect of this architectural diversity is abundant choice – only imagination can limit how you live in the metropolis.

London's historical vicissitudes have etched a unique character onto both its inhabitants and its landscape. In the current economic boom the city appears vibrant. The greyness of past decades of financial gloom has lifted and a new positive outlook is reflected in a surge of ambitious building projects and urban renewal. London hasn't experienced such an overwhelming sense of optimism and confidence since it was swinging in the sixties. In the international arena today it is the capital of capitals, combining its position as a major financial centre with a justified reputation as one of the world's creative hot spots. Like many large cities, London is a series of insular

Londres a toujours été une ville fascinante mais, à l'aube de ce nouveau millénaire, le pouvoir magnétique qu'elle exerce sur notre imagination est particulièrement puissant. Ses nombreux pôles d'attraction sont aussi variés que la ville elle-même, mais elle est également réputée pour être peu accueillante, une ville d'initiés peuplée de Londoniens dédaigneux et hautains. Ceci dit, cette célèbre froideur fait probablement partie de ses attraits, surtout pour ceux qui y viennent attirés par son image de creuset des arts, de la mode et de la musique. Percer à Londres est devenu le dernier défi des créatifs.

Aujourd'hui, Londres est portée par une vague d'optimisme économique et de résurgence de créativité. Toutefois, historiquement, elle a toujours été en mutation et en régénération perpétuelle. Elle a surgi des berges de la Tamise il y a plus de 2 000 ans pour devenir la métropole gigantesque qu'elle est aujourd'hui, dominant le sud-ouest de l'Angleterre. Contrairement à Paris ou à Rome, elle n'a jamais connu de grands projets d'urbanisation. Elle a évolué de façon organique, par vagues sporadiques de développement immobilier dictées par les marées montantes et descendantes de l'économie.

Cette régénération constante a créé un paysage urbain changeant continuellement. Au nom du progrès, les Victoriens en mal de modernisation rasèrent à tire-larigot les églises et les bâtiments jugés trop anciers. Selon le goût de chacun, le résultat est une ville de contrastes débordante de vie ou un bric-à-brac sans queue ni tête de styles architecturaux. Néanmoins, cette diversité architecturale a un effet secondaire bénéfique: l'abondance du choix.

Les aléas historiques de la ville ont donné à ses habitants un caractère aussi particulier que son aspect. Dans le boom économique actuel, Londres déborde d'énergie. La grisaille du marasme financier des décennies antérieures s'est dissipée pour laisser place à un positivisme qui se reflète dans le déferlement de grands projets architecturaux et dans le renouvellement de son urbanisme. Elle n'avait pas connu une assurance et un optimisme aussi contagieux depuis qu'elle twistait dans les années 1960. Sur la scène internationale, elle est devenue la capitale des capitales, associant sa position de place

London ist zwar schon immer eine außergewöhnliche und faszinierende Stadt gewesen, doch jetzt, da ein neues Jahrtausend gerade begonnen hat, hält sie die Fantasie und Vorstellungskraft der Menschen mit besonderer Anziehungskraft gefangen. Die unterschiedlichsten Attraktionen sind so reichhaltig und groß wie die Stadt selbst. Es genießt allerdings auch den Ruf, ein unfreundlicher Ort zu sein, eine Stadt für Insider, bewohnt von arroganten Londonern, die auf andere herabblicken. Aber man kann auch einwenden, dass gerade diese schon berüchtigte Unnahbarkeit eine der Attraktionen der Stadt ist. Sich die Stadt zu erobern – das ist sicherlich die größte kreative Herausforderung.

Zur Zeit erlebt London gerade eine Blütezeit des wirtschaftlichen Optimismus und der wieder auflebenden Kreativität. Im Gegensatz zu Paris oder Rom existierte hier nie eine große städtebauliche Vision. Stattdessen hat sich London organisch entwickelt, in sporadischen Wellen der Stadterschließung, die den Höhen und Tiefen der Wirtschaftsentwicklung unterlag. Daraus ergibt sich entweder eine pulsierende Stadt voller unerwarteter Konstraste oder ein ungleicher Mischmasch architektonischer Ausrichtungen – je nachdem, auf welcher Seite man bei dieser Diskussion steht. Doch auf jeden Fall hat diese architektonische Vielfalt auch eine generelle Buntheit geschaffen.

Die historischen Schicksalsschläge haben der Stadtlandschaft London und dem Charakter ihrer Bewohner etwas ganz Außergewöhnliches verliehen. Im heutigen Wirtschaftsboom zeigt die Stadt eine äußerst lebendige Präsenz. Ein derart überwältigendes Gefühl von Optimismus und Selbstvertrauen hat London seit seinen »swinging sixties« nicht mehr ausgestrahlt. Heute ist die Stadt in der internationalen Arena die Hauptstadt aller Hauptstädte und vereint ihre Position als bedeutendes Finanzzentrum mit dem Image, einer der kreativsten Orte der ganzen Welt zu sein.

Wie viele andere Großstädte hat sich auch London aus einer Aneinanderreihung kleiner Inselchen mit Dorfcharakter gebildet. Welches dieser Dörfer sich der Einzelne aussucht und für welchen Architekturstil er sich entscheidet, sagt in dieser

Brick Lane, London E1

Saville Row, London W1

villages. It is possible to cross from one side of the street to the other and enter a completely different world. The long-standing artistic and Bangladeshi communities that live side by side around the Brick Lane area in the East End are a moment away from the throbbing financial heart of the City, while Islington in the north is known for its desirable and elegant flat-fronted Georgian terraces within yards of sprawling concrete public housing.

Your village and architecture of choice can say an awful lot about the kind of person you are in this city. Assumptions are easily made on the strength of a postcode alone. An SW6 (Fulham) postcode conjures up images of 30-something "smug-marrieds" (a term coined by Helen Fielding in her "Bridget Jones" novels); W11 (Notting Hill) is heaving with "trendier than trustafarians" (they have a private income but look like ragamuffins); and EC1 (Clerkenwell) is populated by that archetypally 1990s phenomenon, the urban loft-dweller. But things are not quite that simple. The continually shifting sands of fashion mean that these interpretations are also in a state of flux. Thus, for example, while Notting Hill in the 1980s was considered the epitome of multicultural bohemianism, today it is being called "the new Chelsea", and the run-down areas of Hoxton and Shoreditch in the east are now, confusingly, "the new Notting Hill". Chelsea's King's Road meanwhile, which in its sixties heyday was the equivalent of Hoxton, is now bona fide establishment.

As the 1990s media and marketing phenomenon "lifestyle" becomes more pervasive and egalitarian, the resolutely fashionable Londoner has been forced to look further afield and be even more inventive to stay ahead of the crowd. There is hardly an area in central London which hasn't been "discovered", which leaves only one way to go. It's odds on that suburbia will be the next Big Thing.

London is an extraordinary city – endlessly creative and imaginative, vibrant and contradictory, multiculturally unique, paradoxically sophisticated and iconoclastic, sometimes eccentric, but always intriguing. This book is a window on the private worlds of a handful of Londoners whose homes reflect the city in all its spirited diversity.

forte financière à la réputation justifiée d'être l'un des lieux les plus créatifs actuellement.

Comme de nombreuses autres grandes villes, elle est composée de villages à la personnalité bien marquée. Les communautés artistiques et bangladaises qui se partagent depuis longtemps le quartier de Brick Lane ne sont qu'à deux pas du cœur financier de la City. Au nord, les élégants et très huppés alignements de façades du 18e siècle d'Islington côtoient des kilomètres de H.L.M. en béton.

Dans cette ville, votre village et votre architecture de prédilection en disent long sur la personne que vous êtes. Un simple code postal peut inspirer des conclusions hâtives. SW6 (Fulham) évoque immédiatement des images de jeunes trentenaires «fièrement mariés» – une expression d'Helen Fielding dans ses journaux de «Bridget Jones». W11 (Notting Hill) grouille de banquiers rastaquouères dans le vent (ils sont pleins aux as mais ont l'air de va-nu-pieds). EC1 (Clerkenwell) est l'antre de ce phénomène typique des années 1990, le «lofteur urbain». Mais les choses ne sont pas aussi simples. Les sables mouvants de la mode rendent ces interprétations des plus fluctuantes. Dans les années 1980, Notting Hill était synonyme de bohème cosmopolite. Aujourd'hui, on l'appelle «la nouvelle Chelsea» tandis que les quartiers délabrés d'Hoxton et de Shoreditch, à l'est, sont devenus «les nouveaux Notting Hill». De son côté, la King's Road à Chelsea, qui était l'équivalent d'Hoxton dans les années 1960, incarne désormais l'establishment.

A mesure que le phénomène médiatique et commercial du «dis moi comment tu vis et je te dirai qui tu es» des années 1990 se répand et se démocratise, le Londonien branché est contraint de regarder toujours un peu plus loin et de redoubler d'imagination pour se démarquer de la masse.

Londres est une ville énergique et contradictoire, d'un multiculturalisme unique en son genre, paradoxalement sophistiquée et iconoclaste, parfois excentrique mais toujours intrigante. Ce livre est une fenêtre ouverte sur les mondes privés d'une poignée de Londoniens dont les intérieurs reflètent la ville dans toute sa diversité inspirée.

Stadt eine ganze Menge über ihn aus. Man neigt schnell dazu, Vermutungen über eine Person nur auf Grund des »postcode« anzustellen: Der Stadtteil SW6 (Fulham) steht für über 30 und »selbstzufrieden-verheiratet«, wie es die englische Erfolgsautorin Helen Fielding in ihren »Bridget Jones«-Romanen beschreibt. Der Stadtteil W11 (Notting Hill) hingegen ist mit den »trustafarians« bevölkert, die über eben einen »trust fund« oder sonstigen reichen Geldgeber verfügen und sich deswegen den Chic von Kanalratten leisten können. EC1 (Clerkenwell) wiederum wird von einem Phänomen belebt, das archetypisch für die 1990er Jahre war: dem städtischen Loftbewohner. Aber ganz so einfach ist es dann doch nicht. Der Treibsand, auf dem alles steht, was Mode und Trend bestimmt, sorgt dafür, dass sich solche Interpretationen immer in Bewegung befinden. So verkörperte Notting Hill in den 1980er Jahren noch den Multikulti-Bohemien. Heute nennt man den Stadtteil schon »das neue Chelsea«, und längst haben ihm Hoxton und Shoreditch im heruntergewirtschafteten Osten der Stadt als »neues Notting Hill« den Rang abgelaufen. Die King's Road in Chelsea war in den 1960er Jahren das, was Hoxton heute ist. Sie gehört nun mit Haut und Haaren zum Establishment.

Je mehr sich der Medien- und Marketing-Lifestyle als Phänomen durchsetzt, desto mehr sind die wirklich modebewussten Londoner gezwungen, weit über ihren Tellerrand zu blicken und immer erfindungsreicher zu werden, wollen sie die Nase beim Trendsetten weiter vorne haben.

London ist eine außergewöhnliche Stadt. Sie ist lebendig und widersprüchlich, ist einzigartig multikulturell, auf paradoxe Weise gleichzeitig kultiviert und bilderstürmerisch bewegt, ist manchmal exzentrisch, aber immer faszinierend. Dieses Buch soll wie ein Fenster den Blick in die Privatwelt einiger Londoner ermöglichen, deren Wohnungen und Häuser die Stadt in ihrer ganzen temperamentvollen Vielseitigkeit widerspiegeln.

Saville Row, London W1

Hassan Abdullah, Michel Lasserre et Stefan Karlson sont trois amis qui travaillent et vivent ensemble, un peu comme les Nations unies avec Hassan dans le rôle du secrétaire général. Ils partagent leur pub victorien près de Liverpool Street avec une ménagerie, réelle et empaillée, aux origines également multiples. Ils l'ont acheté après qu'il ait été squatté, et la tâche colossale de restauration et de décoration est un travail en évolution perpétuelle. Mais même s'ils achevaient les travaux, le décor continuerait de changer car il sert de vitrine aux meubles et aux œuvres d'art que vendent les trois amis. Naturellement, Hassan détient un droit de veto sur la décoration et estime que « les gens ne se laissent pas suffisamment aller. Notre maison est l'expression de notre personnalité mais elle serait encore plus extravagante si j'y vivais seul ». A ce point, on peut entendre Michel ajouter par derrière : « On se demande jusqu'où il pourrait aller ! »

Hassan Abdullah, Michel Lasserre & Stefan Karlson

Hassan Abdullah, Michel Lasserre and Stefan Karlson are friends who work together and live together – it's all rather like the United Nations, with Hassan as the self-proclaimed Secretary General. Their Victorian pub near Liverpool Street is shared with a menagerie of animals, both real and stuffed, whose origins are equally multinatural. Bought after it had been squatted in, the monumental task of restoration and decoration is ongoing, but even if it were finished one day, it would still change continuously as a showcase for the furniture and art the trio sell. Naturally Hassan has the power to veto anything he thinks doesn't quite work and believes "People should be less restrained. Our house is an expression of ourselves, but it would be even more flamboyant if I lived alone." At which point Michel can just be heard saying: "That would be going too far!"

Hassan Abdullah, Michel Lasserre und Stefan Karlson sind Freunde, die auch zusammen arbeiten und leben. Ihre Lebensgemeinschaft erinnert an die Vereinten Nationen – mit Hassan Abdullah als selbst ernanntem Generalsekretär. Ihren viktorianischen Pub nahe der Liverpool Street teilen sie sich mit einem ganzen Zoo aus teils echten, teils ausgestopften Tieren, die ebenfalls aus den unterschiedlichsten Ländern stammen. Gekauft haben sie den Pub, nachdem dort Hausbesetzer gehaust hatten. Die monumentale Aufgabe des Restaurierens und Dekorierens ist noch in vollem Gange, doch selbst wenn sie eines Tages abgeschlossen sein sollte, würde sich die Wohnung dennoch weiterhin verändern – dank der Möbel und Kunstwerke, die das Trio hier verkauft. Und natürlich macht Hassan Abdullah von seinem Vetorecht Gebrauch, wenn er das Gefühl hat, etwas würde nicht funktionieren: »Die Menschen sollten expressiver sein. Das Haus drückt zwar unsere Persönlichkeit aus, aber wenn ich hier allein leben würde, wäre es noch viel extravaganter!« An diesem Punkt des Gesprächs hört man Michel Lasserre murmeln: »und das wäre dann des Guten zuviel!«

First page: *the living room on the first floor. A 19th-century Italian table is surrounded by gold-embroidered Middle Eastern velvet floor cushions. The columns are Russian and the chandelier is Swedish.*
Left: *the Victorian interior of the bar, which doubles up as a grand dining room and ultimate party venue. Murano glass ceiling lamps, originally designed for a restaurant in France, dominate the space.*
Above: *Hassan, Michel, Stefan, Max & Oscar the Dalmatians and a crocodile called Quentin in front of the pub's restored gilded Victorian glass panels.*

Première page: *le salon du premier étage. Une table italienne 19ᵉ est entourée de coussins en velours brodé d'or venant du Moyen Orient. Les deux colonnes en bois doré sont russes et le lustre suédois.*
A gauche: *la salle de bar victorienne sert de salle à manger d'apparat et accueille des fêtes au tonnerre. Des lustres en verre de Murano, conçus à l'origine pour un restaurant en France, dominent la scène.*
Ci-dessus: *Hassan, Michel, Stefan, les dalmatiens Max et Oscar, et Quentin le crocodile devant les panneaux de verre du pub victorien.*

Eingangsseite: *das Wohnzimmer im ersten Stock. Um einen italienischen Tisch aus dem 19. Jahrhundert liegen goldbestickte Samtkissen aus dem Nahen Osten. Die beiden vergoldeten Säulen stammen aus Russland, der Kronleuchter aus Schweden.*
Links: *Die viktorianische Bar fungiert gleichzeitig als prunkvolles Esszimmer und ultimativer Partyraum. Deckenlampen aus MuranoGlas in zartem Rosa beherrschen den Raum.*
Oben: *Hassan, Michel, Stefan, die Dalmatiner Max und Oscar sowie Quentin, das Krokodil, vor den restaurierten Glasplatten mit Goldschrift des viktorianischen Pubs.*

Right: Hassan decided to make all their stuffed animals into royalty and almost all of them now have a crown, tiara or sparkling head-dress. This tiger has a diamanté skirt draped around its ears, while "Bambi" wears his tiara around his neck as he's so tiny. Behind is a French 1970s backlit glass mosaic panel, while the English oak sideboard is in neo-Gothic style.

Below: Layers of paint were stripped to reveal pink hues, which complement the colour of the raw plaster. The mahogany painted bar will eventually be restored back to the original wood. The huge fob watch was from the New York Tiffany's.

A droite: Hassan a décidé d'anoblir tous leurs animaux. A présent, ils ont presque tous une couronne, une tiare ou quelque autre coiffe étincelante. Ce tigre est coiffé d'une jupette en strass tandis que «Bambi», dont la tête est trop frêle, porte sa tiare autour du cou. A l'arrière-plan, une mosaïque en verre éclairée par derrière au-dessus d'un buffet anglais néogothique en chêne.

Ci-dessous: Le décapage de nombreuses couches de peinture a révélé des tons rosés qui s'harmonisent parfaitement avec le plâtre brut. Le bar en acajou peint retrouvera un jour son aspect naturel. L'énorme montre de gousset vient de la boutique new-yorkaise de Tiffany's.

Rechts: Hassan Abdullah beschloss, alle Tiere zu Royals zu machen. Nun trägt fast jedes von ihnen eine Krone, eine Tiara oder anderen funkelnden Kopfschmuck. Diesem Tiger wurde ein Strass-Gehänge über die Ohren gelegt, während »Bambi« seine Tiara um den schlanken Hals trägt. Dahinter steht ein von hinten beleuchtetes Paneel aus Glasmosaik, das in den 1970er Jahren in Frankreich gefertigt wurde. Das neugotische Sideboard aus Eiche ist englischen Ursprungs.

Unten: Lage um Lage wurde die Wandfarbe abgetragen, bis sich Schattierungen in zartem Rosa offenbarten, die gut zur Farbe des unbearbeiteten Mörtels passten. Die in einem Mahagoniton gestrichene Bar wird bald wieder ihre ursprüngliche Holzfarbe erhalten. Die riesige Taschenuhr stammt von Tiffany's, New York.

Above: A fur blanket made from French mountain goat covers a pile of salvaged wood flooring which is waiting to be laid in the living room. Above, among the menagerie of animal heads, is a very rare "Marco Polo's goat" from the Himalayas. The 19th-century French wrought-iron lantern is one of the first things Hassan bought when he started dealing in Camden Market.
Right: Set in a dark wall recess in the pub is a Victorian stuffed bulldog which, because fashions change, is physically very different from the breed today.

Ci-dessus: Une couverture française en chamois recouvre une pile de lattes de parquet qui attendent d'être posées dans le salon. Parmi la collection de trophées de chasse, une très rare tête de «chèvre de Marco Polo», venant de l'Himalaya. La lanterne française du 19e siècle en fer forgé est l'un des premiers objets achetés par Hassan lorsqu'il a commencé à chiner sur le marché de Camden.
A droite: Dans un recoin sombre du pub, un bouledogue empaillé de l'époque victorienne, qui, du fait de l'évolution des modes, est très différent de la race actuelle.

Oben: Eine Decke aus dem Fell französischer Bergziegen deckt einen Stapel alter Bohlen ab, die nun auf ihre Verlegung im Wohnzimmer warten. In der Menagerie von Tierköpfen befindet sich auch eine äußerst seltene »Marco-Polo-Ziege« aus dem Himalaja. Die schmiedeeiserne französische Laterne aus dem 19. Jahrhundert gehört zu den ersten Stücken, die Hassan Abdullah kaufte, nachdem er einen Stand in Camden Market eröffnet hatte.
Rechts: In einer dunklen Nische im Pub befindet sich eine viktorianische ausgestopfte Bulldogge. Sie unterscheidet sich physisch auffallend von den heutigen Hundezüchtungen, weil Moden ja ständig wechseln.

Clockwise from top left: *An 18th-century Italian giltwood sunburst dominates the midnight-blue bedroom; a lacquered mahogany lift from the Savoy hotel will become a bathroom when the chinoiserie ceramic toilet and sink are plumbed in; sunburst clocks and mirrors echo the huge sunburst in the bedroom and the 1960s floor rug; the sundial in the bathroom is in line with the skylight above.*

Du haut à gauche, dans le sens des aiguilles d'une montre: *Un soleil italien en bois doré du 18ᵉ siècle domine la chambre bleu nuit; cet ascenseur en acajou laqué provenant de l'hôtel Savoy et sera trans-* *formé en salle de bain; des horloges et des miroirs dorés en forme de soleil font écho au tapis des années 1960; le cadran solaire dans la salle de bains s'accorde bien avec la verrière du plafond.*

Im Uhrzeigersinn von links oben: *Ein vergoldeter italienischer Sonnenkranz aus dem 18. Jahrhundert beherrscht das dunkelblaue Schlafzimmer; ein Lift aus lackiertem Mahagoni aus dem Savoy-Hotel wird zum Bad; Strahlenkränze nehmen das Motiv des Teppichs aus den 1960er Jahren auf; die Sonnenuhr im Badezimmer ist auf das darüber liegende Dachfenster ausgerichtet.*

London Interiors   Hassan Abdullah, Michel Lasserre & Stefan Karlson

The "den" on the living-room floor is a shrine to Hassan's love of 1960s and 1970s furniture. As they all agreed that a large television was a must, rather than try to blend it into the classical style of the living room, they made it the focus of this more cosy area.

«L'antre», dans un coin du salon au premier étage, est un hommage à l'amour que porte Hassan au mobilier des années 1960 et 1970. Ayant convenu qu'un grand téléviseur était de rigueur, ils en ont fait le point central de leur petit nid douillet plutôt que d'essayer de le fondre dans le style classique du salon.

Das Herrenzimmer auf der Wohnetage ist Hassans persönlicher »Schrein«, seiner Liebe zu Möbeln aus den 1960er und 1970er Jahren gewidmet. Da sich alle darüber im Klaren waren, dass ein riesiger Fernseher ein Muss ist, versuchte man erst gar nicht, ihn optisch in das klassisch ausgerichtete Wohnzimmer einzupassen, sondern machte ihn zum Mittelpunkt dieses kuscheligen Bereichs.

Lorsque l'artiste Nicholas Alvis Vega et la styliste de mode Liza Bruce
ont emménagé dans cet atelier de 95 mètres carrés à Kensington, ils
en ont profité pour se débarrasser de pratiquement tous les meubles de
leur ancienne maison. Aujourd'hui, ils vivent dans un univers intros-
pectif de leur cru, tout en couleurs pures. «Ce qu'il y a de spécial dans
cet endroit», explique Alvis Vega, «c'est qu'il est fermé, caché là où on
s'attend à trouver un jardin derrière un alignement de maisons».
Construit avant la Première Guerre mondiale pour héberger la cha-
pelle d'une école du silence, le bâtiment a ensuite accueilli une école
de danse jusque dans les années 1960. Vivre et travailler dans un
même lieu convient bien au couple. «Liza se lève souvent à 2 heures
du matin pour se mettre à sa planche à dessin, ce qu'elle peut faire
ici», explique Nicholas. «Nous ne pourrions pas travailler séparés l'un
de l'autre. Vivre d'une autre façon serait un compromis».

Nicholas Alvis Vega & Liza Bruce

When artist Nicholas Alvis Vega and fashion designer Liza Bruce
moved into this 1,000-square-foot Kensington studio, they got rid
of almost everything from their previous home. Today they live in
an inward-looking colour-box world of their own creation. "The
special thing about this place," explains Alvis Vega, "is that it is enclosed, hidden away where there would normally be gardens behind a row of houses." Built before the First World War as the
chapel of a school of silence, it was a dance school until the 1960s.
They have found that living and working in one space suits them:
"Liza often gets up at 2am to work, she can do that here," he explains. "I can't think how we'd work apart," he says; "living any
other way would be a compromise."

Als der Künstler Nicholas Alvis Vega und die Modedesignerin Liza
Bruce in dies 95 Quadratmeter großes Studio in Kensington zogen,
entledigten sie sich fast aller Dinge ihrer früheren Wohnungen. Heute
leben sie in einer nach innen gewandten Farbschachtel, die sie zu ihrer eigenen, ganz persönlichen Welt gemacht haben. »Das Besondere
an diesem Ort ist«, erläutert Alvis Vega, »dass er eine verborgene Enklave ist. Normalerweise befinden sich hier die Gärten von Reihen-
häusern.« Vor dem Ersten Weltkrieg als Kapelle einer »school of
silence« errichtet, war es bis in die 1960er Jahre eine Tanzschule. In
ein und derselben Wohnung leben und arbeiten – das ist für das Paar
kein Problem. »Lisa steht oft nachts um zwei Uhr auf, um zu arbeiten, was Sie hier gut tun kann«, erzählt er. »Ich kann mir gar nicht
vorstellen, wie das wäre, wenn wir getrennt arbeiten würden. Alles
andere wäre für uns nur ein Kompromiss.«

Clockwise from top left: *A painted mirror smeared with Vaseline stands at the foot of the bed, piles of 1960s Playboy magazines are stacked to the left and the bed is covered in a "psychedelic Genghis Khan" patchwork quilt of lambskins; an elephant's skull rests on a wooden African stool; a collection of objects on a Gio Ponti sideboard includes glasswork by Alvis Vega.*

Du haut à gauche, dans le sens des aiguilles d'une montre: *au pied du lit, un miroir peint maculé de vaseline. Sur la gauche, des piles de «Playboy» des années 1960; le lit est recouvert d'un patchwork en peaux d'agneaux intitulé «Gengis Khan psychédélique»; un crâne d'éléphant sur un tabouret africain en bois; sur une console de Gio Ponti, une collection d'objets dont des verreries d'Alvis Vega.*

Im Uhrzeigersinn von links oben: *Am Fußende des Bettes steht ein bemalter und mit Vaseline beschmierter Spiegel. Auf dem Bett liegt ein »psychedelischer Dschingis Khan« – ein Patchwork-Quilt aus Lammfell; ein Elefantenschädel thront auf einem afrikanischen Stuhl; zu der Sammlung auf dem Sideboard von Gio Ponti gehören auch Glasarbeiten von Alvis Vega.*

London Interiors   Nicholas Alvis Vega & Liza Bruce

Bruce and Alvis Vega have an obsession with colour. His graduated "colour field" paintings, which adorn both the studio and her Chelsea shop, are taken from household paint charts. The studio walls had previously been painted in the palest of pink with marble dust vertical stripes until one morning Alvis got up and covered them in what he refers to as "park-keeper's hut green".

Bruce et Alvis Vega sont des obsédés de la couleur. Les «Champs de couleurs gradués» d'Alvis Vega, qui ornent son atelier ainsi que la boutique de Bruce, s'inspirent des nuanciers de peintures murales. Les murs de l'atelier étaient rose très pâle avec des rayures verticales en poudre de marbre jusqu'au matin où, au saut du lit, Alvis les a recouverts de ce qu'il appelle «un vert de cabane de garde forestier».

Liza Bruce und Nicholas Alvis Vega sind Farbfetischisten. Seine »Colour field«-Gemälde bestechen durch feine Farbabstufungen. Die Studiowände waren ursprünglich in einem hauchzarten Pinkton gestrichen und mit vertikalen Streifen aus Marmorstaub verziert, bis Alvis eines Morgens aufstand und sie in dem Grünton strich, den man sonst an den Försterhäuschen der Parks findet.

Westbourne Grove, London W11

Solange Azagury-Partridge est un de ces êtres que l'on envie, une femme qui a une foi inébranlable en son propre goût. Alors que le tout Londres se parait de vert glacé et de minimalisme à la Prada, Solange dessinait son showroom de bijoux comme elle l'entendait, sans se soucier des modes. Cinq ans plus tard, son intérieur décadent tapissé de velours est toujours d'actualité...pour ceux qui attachent de l'importance à une chose aussi futile que la mode. «Je ne vais pas modifier mon style de vie pour me conformer à une tendance», affirme-t-elle. «En outre, quand j'examine ces tendances prétendument nouvelles dans des revues, j'y retrouve toujours des éléments que j'ai déjà intégrés». Tout comme les souliers Manolo Blahnik, les cachemires moulants et les Levis indigo qu'elle a adoptés, les intérieurs de Solange sont funky mais chic. De son appartement de Paddington, elle déclare: «Avant tout, il faut que ce soit comme une vraie maison. J'adore le chaos que créent les enfants. Il s'agit d'un espace de vie.»

Solange Azagury-Partridge

Solange Azagury-Partridge is that enviable thing – a woman who has utter faith in her own taste. When the rest of London was going all Prada ice-green and minimal, Solange designed her jewellery showroom exactly how she wanted it, regardless of fashion. That decadent velvet padded interior is still, five years on, bang up to the minute – that is, if you care about such a fickle thing as fashion. "I won't change the way I live to accommodate a trend," she says, "and besides, when I look at all those so-called new trends in design magazines, I always have an element of it already." Like the Manolo Blahnik kitten heels, slinky cashmere and indigo Levis she favours, Solange's interiors are funky but stylish. "It's all about feeding the senses," she explains. Of her family's Paddington flat she maintains, "above all, it must feel like a home. I love the chaos the kids bring to my life; home has to be a living environment."

Solange Azagury-Partridge ist beneidenswert – eine Frau, die ihrem eigenen Geschmack felsenfest vertraut. Als ganz London sich plötzlich dem Pradagrün unreifer Äpfel und dem Minimalismus verschrieb, gestaltete Solange Azagury-Partridge ihren Showroom für den selbst entworfenen Schmuck ganz nach ihrem eigenen Geschmack und völlig modeunabhängig. Fünf Jahre später ist das mit Samt ausgeschlagene, dekadente Interieur immer noch topaktuell – wenn man in den Kategorien der stetig wechselnden Mode denken will. »Ich möchte meinen Lebensstil keinen momentanen Trends unterwerfen«, sagt Solange Azagury-Partridge. »Und wenn ich mir diese so genannten neuen Trends in Designmagazinen anschaue, stelle ich fest, dass Teile daraus bereits in meinem eigenen Stil zu finden sind.« Wie die Manolo-Blahnik-Schuhe, anschmiegsamen Kaschmirstoffe und Indigojeans, die sie gern trägt ist auch ihr Wohnstil. »Alles dreht sich um die Sinne«, erklärt sie. Und die Familienwohnung in Paddington »muss vor allem ein Heim sein. Ich liebe das Chaos, das die Kinder beisteuern. Es muss ein von Leben erfülltes Umfeld sein«.

Westbourne Grove antique dealer Nick Hayward produced the modern Perspex table and chairs based on an older design in Solange's kitchen. The swivel-chair with red leatherette cushions is a 1960s original; the painting above is by friend Julia Warr from her Goldsmiths College degree show.

Nick Hayward, le célèbre antiquaire basé à Westbourne Grove, a déniché la table et les chaises modernes Perspex en se basant sur un design plus ancien dans la cuisine de Solange. Le fauteuil pivotant tapissé en similicuir rouge est une pièce originale des années 1960. Le tableau a

été réalisé par une amie, Julia Warr, pour l'exposition des diplômés de son école, Goldsmiths.

Die Perspex-Stühle und den Tisch in der Küche brachte Nick Hayward, der berühmte Antiquitätenhändler in Westbourne Grove, nach einem älteren Entwurf heraus. Der Drehstuhl mit Kissen aus rotem Kunstleder ist ein Original aus den 1960er Jahren. Das Gemälde darüber fertigte Solanges Freundin Julia Warr als Abschlußarbeit am Goldsmiths College an.

London Interiors   Solange Azagury-Partridge

Solange's son Otis was so unhappy about moving that she decided to paint his room the same blood-orange red that had been in their previous living room, and also put the carpet in there, "to make him feel more at home". On the wall are vivid flower photographs by Michael Banks.

Son fils Otis était si malheureux à l'idée de déménager que Solange a décidé de peindre sa chambre de la même couleur sanguine que leur ancien salon et y a mis le tapis «pour qu'il se sente plus chez lui». Au mur, des photographies de fleurs très colorées de Michael Banks.

Der Gedanke an einen Umzug machte ihren Sohn Otis so unglücklich, dass Solange beschloss, sein Zimmer im gleichen Orangerot zu streichen, in dem das frühere Wohnzimmer gehalten war. Auch den alten Teppich brachte sie mit, »damit er sich mehr zu Hause fühlt«. An der Wand hängen farbenfrohe Blumenfotos von Michael Banks.

Peu de gens peuvent se targuer de vivre dans un chef-d'œuvre de l'architecture, mais c'est pourtant le cas d'Ou Baholyodhin et d'Erez Yardeni. Perché sur le plus haut sommet au nord de Londres, avec une vue sur les cinq comtés de la capitale, leur luxueux appartement de Highpoint Two été dessiné à la fin des années 1930 par Berthold Lubetkin, le père du modernisme britannique et international. Ce fut également sa demeure jusqu'en 1955, quand il décida de fuir la ville et l'architecture pour aller élever des cochons dans le Gloucestershire. Yardeni, peintre et maître d'escrime, et Baholyodhin, créateur de meubles, se considèrent comme les gardiens d'une œuvre d'art plutôt que comme ses propriétaires. Ils ont restauré leur intérieur avec l'aide de l'architecte John Allan, qui est également le biographe de Lubetkin, et ont même retrouvé certains des meubles d'origine.

Ou Baholyodhin & Erez Yardeni

Not many people can claim to live in an architectural masterpiece, but this is undeniably true of the home shared by Ou Baholyodhin and Erez Yardeni. Perched on the highest point above north London with views across five counties, the penthouse at Highpoint Two was designed in the late 1930s by Berthold Lubetkin, the father of British and international Modernism. It was also his home until 1955, when he gave up the city and architecture for a life of pig farming in Gloucestershire. Yardeni, a painter and fencing master, and Baholyodin, a furniture designer, see their role more as caretakers of a work of art rather than as owners of it. The interior has been restored with the help of architect John Allan, who is also Lubetkin's biographer, and even some of the original furniture has been reinstated.

Nur wenige Menschen können von sich behaupten, in einem architektonischen Meisterwerk zu wohnen – doch das ist hier zweifelsfrei der Fall. Ou Baholyodhin und Erez Yardeni leben auf dem höchsten Punkt Nord-Londons mit Blick auf fünf Grafschaften. Ihr Penthouse in Highpoint Two wurde Ende der 1930er Jahre von Berthold Lubetkin entworfen, dem Begründer des britischen und internationalen Modernismus. Bis 1955 war es sein Zuhause, dann gab er Stadt und Architektur auf und wurde Schweinefarmer in Gloucestershire. Erez Yardeni, Maler und Fechtmeister, und Ou Baholyodhin, Möbeldesigner, sehen ihre Rolle nicht so sehr als Besitzer, sondern verstehen sich eher als Bewahrer eines Kunstwerks. Mit Hilfe des Architekten John Allan, der auch der Biograf von Berthold Lubetkin ist, erhielt das Innere wieder sein ursprüngliches Aussehen; sogar einige Originalmöbel wurden zurückgebracht.

Previous pages: *Eight metres of continuous glass and a vast wood-decked terrace provide stunning views across London and a constant awareness of the changing weather outside.*
Right and below: *The flat is planned around this huge central living room showing an expanse of chocolate-coloured ceramic tiles which Lubetkin intended to symbolise ploughed soil with the blue sky above and a dining table and chairs designed by Baholyodhin.*

Double page précédente*: Les huit mètres de baies vitrées ininterrompues et la terrasse parquetée offrent des vues spectaculaires sur Londres. Ici, on est constamment informé des humeurs changeantes du temps.*
A droite*: la salle de séjour vue de la cuisine.*
Ci-dessous*: Tout l'appartement a été conçu autour de cette immense salle de séjour centrale, tapissée de carreaux de céramique couleur chocolat qui, pour Lubetkin, symbolisaient la terre labourée sous un ciel d'azur. La table et les chaises ont été dessinées par Baholyodhin.*

Vorhergehende Doppelseite*: Die acht Meter breite Glaswand und die riesige Terrasse mit Holzboden ermöglichen atemberaubende Ausblicke über London. Gleichzeitig ist man sich jeder Wetterveränderung bewusst.*
Rechts und unten*: Die Wohnung wurde um den riesigen zentralen Wohnbereich herum geplant. Er ist ganz mit schokoladenbraunen Fliesen ausgelegt, die Lubetkin als Symbol der beackerten Erde im Gegensatz zum blauen Himmel darüber gedacht hatte. Esstisch und Stühle gestaltete Ou Baholyodhin.*

Above: On either side of the kitchen entrance is a reinstated photomural of 120 images from the Pollock Toy Theatre. The two cowhide chairs were designed by Lubetkin for the penthouse, while the carpet is a recreation of the original.
Right: Cowhide was often used in Modernist interiors. Baholyodhin designed for the penthouse both the beige suede and wood sofa and the tall wood table, on which is displayed a West African Mummye tribe ritual mask. The moulded fibreglass chair and turned wood stool are by Charles and Ray Eames.

Ci-dessus: De chaque côté de l'entrée de la cuisine, une fresque photographique de 120 images provenant du Pollock Toy Theatre a retrouvé son ancienne place. Les deux fauteuils en vache ont été dessinés par Lubetkin pour l'appartement. Le tapis est une réédition de l'original.
A droite: La peau de vache a souvent été utilisée dans la décoration moderniste. Balayodhin a dessiné le canapé en bois et daim ainsi que la haute table en bois sur laquelle est exposé un masque tribal Mummye d'Afrique occidentale. La chaise en fibres de verre moulée et le tabouret en bois tourné sont de Charles et Ray Eames.

Oben: Zu beiden Seiten der Küchentür befindet sich ein wiederhergestelltes Wandbild aus Fotografien, das 120 Motive aus dem Pollock Toy Theatre zeigt. Die beiden mit Kuhfell bezogenen Sessel sind Lubetkin-Entwürfe für das Penthouse; der Teppich ist eine Neuauflage des Originals.
Rechts: Die Modernisten arbeiteten viel mit Kuhfellen. Baholyodhin entwarf das Sofa aus beigefarbenem Wildleder und Holz. Auch den hohen Holztisch, auf dem eine Ritualmaske des westafrikanischen Stamms der Mummye steht, gestaltete er für das Penthouse. Der Stuhl aus geformtem Fiberglas und der Hocker aus gedrechseltem Holz stammen von Charles und Ray Eames.

Clockwise from top left: *The wall of scorched and sandblasted fir planks is intended to evoke a forest; natural forms and materials are common to both Lubetkin's and Baholyodhin's work; in the entrance foyer, the scorched and sandblasted fir is used to create a "brise soleil"; the kitchen uses cherrywood and travertine, creating continuity with the rest of the penthouse.*

Du haut à gauche, dans le sens des aiguilles d'une montre: *Le mur en planches de sapin brûlées et décapées évoque une forêt; Lubetkin et Baholyodhin préfèrent des formes et des matériels naturels; dans le* vestibule, le sapin brûlé et décapé sert de «brise soleil»; dans la cuisine, le bois de cerisier et le travertin créent une continuité avec le reste de l'appartement.

Im Uhrzeigersinn von links oben: *Die Wand aus Fichtenholz, das gebeizt und gesandstrahlt wurde, soll an einen Wald erinnern; Lubetkin und Baholyodhin bevorzugen natürliche Materialien und Formen; im Eingangsbereich dient das Fichtenholz als »brise soleil«; in der Küche wurden Kirschholz und Travertin verarbeitet, um eine optische Kontinuität mit dem restlichen Penthouse zu erreichen.*

London Interiors Ou Baholyodhin & Erez Yardeni

A wide ledge cut from a single piece of travertine runs the length of the eight-metre window. The rare 17th century Oron tribe wood figure is displayed on a white concrete stand sculpted by Yardeni.

Une corniche taillée dans une seule pièce de travertin court tout le long des huit mètres de fenêtre. Sur une base blanche, sculptée en ciment par Yardeni, est disposée une rare sculpture Oron en bois datant du 17e siècle.

Ein breiter Vorsprung, aus einem einzigen Stück Travertin geschnitten, verläuft entlang des gesamten Fensters mit einer Länge von acht Metern. Die seltene Holzskulptur des Oron-Stammes aus dem 17. Jahrhundert steht auf einem weißen Sockel, den Yardeni aus Zement gestaltet hat.

Facing page: detail of a group of crystal and stone objects displayed by a glass brick window in the kitchen.
Above: view of the bedroom with, in the background, the highly abstract organic design "La Chaise" by Charles and Ray Eames dating from 1948.
Right: The blue tiles in the bathroom evoke the element of water.

Page de gauche: gros plan sur un groupe d'objets en cristal et en pierre disposés dans la cuisine, devant une fenêtre en dalles de verre.
Ci-dessus: vue de la chambre. Devant le mur, «La Chaise», modèle organique de Charles et Ray Eames datant de 1948.
A droite: la salle de bains est tapissée de carreaux de céramique couleur bleue qui évoquent l'eau.

Linke Seite: Detailaufnahme einer Objektgruppe aus Kristall und Stein vor einem Fenster aus Glasbausteinen in der Küche.
Oben: Blick in das Schlafzimmer. Im Hintergrund der organische Stuhl »La Chaise«, den Charles und Ray Eames 1948 entwarfen.
Rechts: Die blauen Kacheln im Badezimmer spielen auf das Element Wasser an.

Les avenues légèrement délabrées et bordées d'arbres de Killburn doivent parfois lui sembler à des années-lumière de la beauté sauvage de son Afrique du Sud natale, pourtant Joel Bernstein se sent chez lui dans cette partie du nord-ouest de Londres. «Pour moi, c'est important de pouvoir contempler un paysage paisible depuis mes fenêtres. Je ne crois pas que je pourrais encore vivre sans jardin». L'adresse n'a peut-être pas le cachet urbain de Hoxton ou de Hackney, par exemple, mais elle fait mouche auprès des amoureux de la nature. La majorité des maisons sont grandes, avec des jardins assortis. L'appartement en sous-sol de Bernstein donne sur une oasis paysagée, avec un apaisant plan de graviers calmes protégé par des bambous et des hêtres. Il a toujours rêvé d'habiter une maison sur une plage et, dans une certaine mesure, c'est ce qu'il a recréé ici. Les matières naturelles utilisées un peu partout et les vastes baies vitrées qui relient l'intérieur à l'extérieur évoquent un style de maisons situées sous des climats plus chauds.

Joel Bernstein

The somewhat shabby tree-lined avenues of Kilburn must at times feel a million miles away from the natural beauty of Joel Bernstein's native South Africa, but it is an area of north-west London he is very happy to call home. "It's important for me to look out onto something peaceful; I don't think I could ever live without a garden again", he explains. While an NW6 address might not have the urbane cachet of say Hoxton or Hackney, it is an ideal postcode for devotees of nature. The majority of houses are large, with gardens to match. Bernstein's basement flat looks out onto a landscaped oasis of calm gravel lawn, sheltered by bamboo and beech trees. He admits to always having dreamt of living in a beach house and to an extent that is what he has created here. Natural materials throughout and large windows connect the interior to the exterior, echoing the style of houses in distant warmer climes.

Ein bisschen heruntergekommen sind die baumbestandenen Hauptstraßen von Kilburn schon. Wenn man wie Joel Bernstein die Naturwunder Südafrikas gewohnt ist, muss man sich hier wie auf einem anderen Planeten fühlen. Aber er wohnt gerne in diesem Stadtteil im Nordwesten Londons. »Ich muss auf etwas Friedliches blicken können. Ich glaube nicht, dass ich noch einmal ohne einen Garten leben könnte«, erklärt er. Mag die Postleitzahl NW6 auch nicht ein urbanes Versteck von der Art der Stadtteile Hoxton or Hackney sein – für Naturfans ist es eine ideale Adresse. Die meisten Häuser sind groß, die dazugehörigen Gärten ebenso. Die Wohnung von Joel Bernstein liegt im Souterrain und eröffnet den Blick auf eine von einem Landschaftsgärtner gestaltete Oase, einen Rasen aus Kies, der beruhigend wirkt und durch Bambus und Buchen geschützt wird. Joel Bernstein wollte schon immer in einem Strandhaus wohnen, und bis zu einem gewissen Grad hat er diesen Traum hier verwirklicht. Es wurden durchgängig natürliche Materialien verwendet und diese schaffen zusammen mit den großen Fenstern eine Verbindung zwischen Innen und Außen, die an den Baustil wärmerer Gefilde erinnert.

First page: *Traditional Ethiopian hardwood chairs are coated in layers of butter to create their rich, dark patina. The airy living room leads off from the entrance hall, but despite the flat having an open-plan feeling the separate spaces are well-defined.*
Above: *A section of the simple galley-style kitchen can be seen from main living room.*

Première page: *Les chaises traditionnelles éthiopiennes en bois dur ont été enduites de nombreuses couches de beurre qui leur donnent cette patine riche et sombre. L'entrée donne directement sur un salon lumineux mais, en dépit de l'impression d'un appartement à plan ouvert, tous les espaces sont bien définis.*
Ci-dessus: *un angle de la petite cuisine de bateau telle qu'on l'aperçoit depuis le salon principal.*

Eingangsseiten: *traditionelle Stühle aus Äthiopien. Die dunkle, intensive Patina wird durch das Einstreichen mit Butter erreicht. Das Wohnzimmer geht vom Eingangsbereich ab. Obwohl die Wohnung sehr offen wirkt, sind die einzelnen Räume klar definiert.*
Oben: *Vom Wohnzimmer aus sieht man einen Teil der kleinen Küche.*

London Interiors   Joel Bernstein

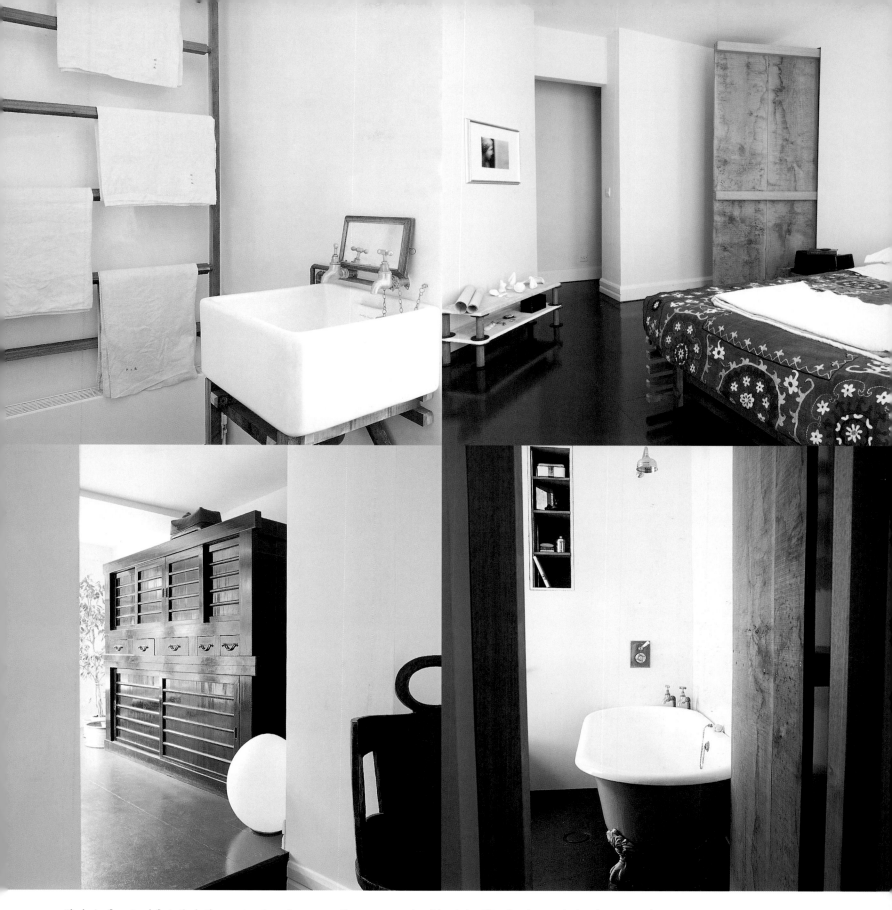

Clockwise from top left: In the bathroom, towels are hung on a rail reminiscent of the climbing bars in a school gymnasium; the bed is covered in a Rajasthan appliqué textile; the pedestal bath stands on sturdy claw-feet; in the second bedroom stands a large 19th-century Japanese cabinet, which would have originally been designed for a traditional town house.

Du haut à gauche, dans le sens des aiguilles d'une montre: Dans la salle de bains, le porte-serviettes évoque les échelles d'un gymnase scolaire; sur le lit, un dessus en appliqué du Rajasthan; la baignoire re-

pose sur de solides pieds griffus; dans la seconde chambre, un grand cabinet japonais du 19ᵉ siècle, sans doute conçu à l'origine pour une maison de ville traditionnelle.

Im Uhrzeigersinn von oben links: Im Bad fühlt man sich beim Anblick des Handtuchhalters an die Sprossenwand in der Schulturnhalle erinnert; auf dem Bett liegt ein bestickter Überwurf aus Rajasthan; die frei stehende Badewanne hat robuste Klauenfüße; im zweiten Schlafzimmer steht ein großer japanischer Schrank aus dem 19. Jahrhundert.

Burlington Gardens, London W1

Ozwald Boateng crée des vêtements pour les hommes qui n'ont pas peur de s'affirmer. Dans le monde rigoureux de la mode masculine, l'impeccable coupe cintrée de ses costumes est reconnaissable entre toutes, tandis que ses tissus traditionnels sont doublés de soies aux couleurs flamboyantes. Son appartement, au-dessus de sa maison de couture sur Wimpole Street, offre la même combinaison inattendue de classicisme rehaussé d'une touche d'excentricité. Boateng, qui met de la couleur à l'intérieur de ses costumes «pour que celui qui les porte se sente bien», applique le même principe chez lui. «L'objectif était de créer une atmosphère relaxante», explique-t-il. «Je ne tiens pas à ramener les tensions du travail chez moi». Avec l'aide de l'artiste et décorateur Kevin Allison, Boateng a réalisé un décor audacieux saupoudré de ses couleurs fétiches, fuchsia, orange et cramoisi. Les peintures murales d'Allison incluent des vagues violettes reposantes dans le salon et des cercles dynamiques dans la cuisine, histoire de se lever du bon pied le matin.

Ozwald Boateng

Ozwald Boateng designs clothes for men who want to say something a little different about themselves. In the exacting world of men's tailoring, Boateng's distinctive suits are cut narrow and sharp and traditional suiting fabrics are lined in brilliant jewel-coloured silks. His home, above his Wimpole Street couture house, is an equally unexpected combination of classical with a colourful twist. Boateng uses colour inside his suits to "make the wearer feel good" and in his home for the similar reason. "The intention was to create a calming atmosphere; it is important that I can leave the stresses of work behind me when I come up here." With artist and designer Kevin Allison, Boateng has created a bold interior suffused with his trademark fuchsia, orange and crimson. Allison's mood-enhancing murals include calming purple waves in the living room and dynamic circles in the kitchen.

Ozwald Boateng entwirft Kleidung für Männer, die sich von der Norm abheben möchten. In der millimetergenauen Welt der Maß-Schneiderei sind Anzüge von Boateng unverwechselbar schmal und sexy-elegant geschnitten, und traditionelle Anzugstoffe werden mit leuchtenden Stoffen unterfüttert, die wie Juwelen schimmern. Auch sein Zuhause, über seinem Couturehaus in der Wimpole Street gelegen, vereint auf ähnlich unerwartete Weise das Klassische mit dem Fröhlich-Bunten. Ozwald Boateng verwendet farbiges Anzugfutter, damit sich die Träger gut fühlen. Aus dem gleichen Grund findet Farbe auch in seinem Zuhause Einsatz. »Ich wollte eine beruhigende Atmosphäre schaffen«, erklärt er. »Es ist wichtig, dass ich hier oben den Stress der Arbeit hinter mir lassen kann.« Zusammen mit dem Künstler und Designer Kevin Allison hat Boateng ein kühnes Interieur geschaffen, durchzogen mit den Farben, die sein Markenzeichen sind: Fuchsia, Orange und Purpur. Allison schuf stimmungshebende Wandmalereien wie die beruhigenden Purpurwellen im Wohnzimmer und dynamische Kreise in der Küche, die als visueller morgendlicher Weckruf gedacht sind.

Above and right: The living room is a surreal mix of sombre Art Deco furnishings and a leather button-back Chesterfield suite against a backdrop of luminous fuchsia pink – a colour scheme not for the faint-hearted, but one that Boateng finds very relaxing. The principles of Feng Shui were considered when planning the design as Boateng felt that "space-clearing" was very important, so the flat is sparsely furnished.
Facing page: In this downstairs showroom, where Boateng is seen reclining on a buckskin sofa, the jagged vertical lines in yellows and golds are intentionally invigorating.

Ci-dessus et à droite: Le salon accueille un assortiment surréaliste de meubles Art Déco sombres et un ensemble de Chesterfields en cuir capitonné se détachant sur un lumineux mur rose fuchsia. C'est une palette détonante que Boateng trouve néanmoins très relaxante. Attachant une grande importance au «vide», il a tenu à conserver un appartement dépouillé, appliquant les principes Feng Shui.
Page de droite: Dans le showroom au rez-de-chaussée, Boateng est assis dans un canapé en daim. Les hachures jaune et or sont intentionnellement revigorantes.

Oben und rechts: Das Wohnzimmer ist ein surrealer Mix aus schwerem Art-Deco-Mobiliar und einem lederbezogenen Chesterfield-Sofa vor einem Hintergrund aus leuchtendem Fuchsia – eine Farbe, für die man durchaus Nerven mitbringen muss, die Ozwald Boateng allerdings als außerordentlich entspannend empfindet. Die Prinzipien des Feng Shui flossen in die Planung ein. Da Boateng den Aspekt des »Leerräumens« für sehr wichtig hielt, gibt es hier auch kaum Mobiliar.
Rechte Seite: Im unteren Showroom entspannt der Hausherr auf einem Wildledersofa. Die gezackten, vertikal verlaufenden Wandmuster in Gelb- und Goldtönen sollen anregend wirken.

Below: The fifth floor houses the bedroom, bathroom and dressing area. Perhaps the boldest colour statement of all can be seen here in a combination of pink, red, rust and gold. It's all very unique; in fact, it's all very Ozwald Boateng.

Ci-dessous: Le cinquième étage abrite la chambre à coucher, la salle de bains et un dressing. Ce dernier arbore sans doute la combinaison de couleurs la plus audacieuse avec ses roses, ses rouges, ses rouilles et ses ors. L'effet est unique. De fait, c'est très Ozwald Boateng.

Unten: Im fünften Stock liegen Schlaf- und Badezimmer sowie der Ankleidebereich. Das vielleicht kühnste Farbarrangement findet sich hier: eine Mischung aus Pink, Rot, Rost und Gold. Unverwechselbar und damit auch typisch für Ozwald Boateng.

Facing page: Allison used the "closed dynamic of the concentric circle" in the design of the kitchen. While much of the flat is decorated in reds and purples, yellow was used in the kitchen in the hope that it would be stimulating at the time it is needed most – in the morning.
Above: Just as Boateng bucks convention in his work, so he also refuses to run with the crowd at home. The rich pink duvet cover is, he says, "a deeply sensual colour"; above it hangs a Chinese lantern, while the red lacquer table completes the exotic boudoir effect.

Page de gauche: Dans la cuisine, Allison a utilisé le motif de «la dynamique fermée des cercles concentriques». Si le reste de l'appartement est surtout décoré en rouges et violets, cette pièce a été peinte en tons jaunes dans l'espoir qu'elle serait stimulante au moment où on en a le plus besoin: au réveil.
Ci-dessus: Luttant contre le conformisme dans son travail, Boateng refuse également le conventionnalisme chez lui. Le duvet rose profond est, dit-il «d'une couleur très sensuelle». Au-dessus du lit, une lanterne chinoise. La table de chevet en laque rouge complète l'effet de boudoir exotique.

Linke Seite: Kevin Allison setzte die »geschlossene Dynamik konzentrischer Kreise« in der Küche ein. Im Gegensatz zu der restlichen Wohnung, die größtenteils in Rot- und Lilatönen gehalten ist, wurde in der Küche die Farbe Gelb verwendet, in der Hoffnung, dass sie dann anregend wirkt, wenn es am nötigsten ist – nämlich morgens.
Oben: Nicht nur in seiner Arbeit, auch in seinem Zuhause hält Boateng es gerne etwas anders als die Konkurrenz. Die Bettdecke ist in einem intensiven Pinkton gehalten, »einer äußerst sinnlichen Farbe«. Darüber hängt eine chinesische Laterne, und der rote Lacktisch vervollständigt das Gefühl, in einem exotischen Boudoir zu sein.

Grand Union Canal, London NW1

Above: If you're not familiar with living on boats, it's always a surprise how much interior space they have, which is because so much of them is hidden beneath the waterline. An 85-foot boat, like The Catharina, has a beam of 22 feet, which means the living room is more generous than that of most London flats. An open-plan kitchen area and lots of rooflight hatches and portholes add to the feeling of spaciousness, even though ceilings are comparatively low.
Left: The wheelhouse is done up in the same style as the below-deck accommodation.

Ci-dessus: Lorsqu'on n'est pas habitué à vivre sur un bateau, on est toujours surpris par la taille de l'espace habitable, en grande partie parce que tout est caché sous la ligne de flottaison. Avec ses 26 mètres de long et ses sept mètres de large, la Catharina a un salon bien plus vaste que la plupart des appartements londoniens. La cuisine ouverte et la lumière qui filtre généreusement à travers les écoutilles et les hublots ajoutent à l'impression d'espace, bien que le plafond soit bas.
A gauche: La timonerie est décorée dans le même style que le pont inférieur.

Oben: Wer das Leben auf einem Hausboot nicht kennt, ist immer wieder überrascht, wie viel Platz man auf so einem Boot hat, denn ein großer Teil liegt verborgen unter der Wasseroberfläche. Ein 26-Meter-Boot wie die Catharina beispielsweise hat eine Breite von fast sieben Metern und damit ein Wohnzimmer, das größer ist als das in den meisten Wohnungen Londons. Eine offene Küche und viele Dachluken und Buglöcher verstärken das Gefühl der räumlichen Großzügigkeit, obwohl die Decken verhältnismäßig niedrig sind.
Links: Das Ruderhaus ist im gleichen Stil eingerichtet wie die darunter liegenden Wohnräume.

L'un des aspects les plus déroutants de Londres est le peu de cas que l'on fait de son fleuve. Alors que la vie parisienne gravite autour de la Seine et que les canaux d'Amsterdam accueillent une vaste communauté d'habitations flottantes, la Tamise s'écoule dans toute sa grisaille, négligée et méprisée par la majorité des Londoniens. Toutefois, les quelques originaux qui osent se mouiller sont rarement déçus. Pour le prix d'un deux-pièces dans le West End, on peut acheter une grande péniche aménagée telle que la Catharina, ancrée à Kew. La perspective de longs hivers froids et humides en décourage probablement plus d'un, alors qu'en fait, les points de mouillage sont tous équipés d'eau courante, du gaz, de l'électricité et de systèmes d'égout semblables à ceux de la terre ferme. En outre, les inconvénients sont largement compensés par les avantages. Ou d'autre peut-on se réveiller le matin devant une vue si dégagée, au grand air et dans l'intimité et le silence relatif d'un fleuve?

The Catharina

One of the perplexing things about London is how little is made of its river. While Paris life centres around the Seine and the waterways of Amsterdam are home to a thriving houseboat community, the Thames meanders grey, neglected and ignored by the majority of Londoners. But the few who do decide to take to the water are rarely disappointed by the experience. For the price of a two-bedroom flat in West London it is possible to buy a large converted barge, like The Catharina, which is moored in Kew. While the prospect of cold damp winters and dubious plumbing probably puts off the majority, in reality moorings are connected to the main water, electricity, gas and sewerage systems – no different from a land dwelling. Besides, any downsides are far outweighed by the upsides. Where else is it possible to wake up to wide-open horizons, clean air and the relative privacy and silence of the river?

Verblüffend an London ist, wie wenig die Einwohner ihren Fluss nutzen. Während sich das Stadtleben in Paris rund um die Seine abspielt und die Grachten Amsterdams eine äußerst lebendige Hausboot-Gemeinde beherbergen, windet sich die Themse in eher grauen Farbtönen und wird von der Mehrheit der Londoner vernachlässigt oder sogar ignoriert. Die wenigen, die sich für ein Leben auf dem Fluss entscheiden, werden allerdings selten enttäuscht. Für den Preis einer 3-Zimmer-Wohnung in West-London kann man sich eine riesige umgebaute Barkasse wie die Catharina leisten, die in Kew vor Anker liegt. Mag die Aussicht auf klamme kalte Winter und eine improvisierte Entsorgung der Abwässer die meisten abschrecken, sieht die Realität anders aus, denn die Ankerplätze sind mit den Hauptwasser-, Elektrizitäts-, Gas- und Abwasserleitungen verbunden, genau so wie eine Wohnung an Land. Außerdem wiegen die Vorteile die Nachteile bei weitem auf. Wo sonst kann man mit Blick auf einen unverbauten Himmel aufwachen, saubere Luft atmen und ein gewisses Maß an Privatsphäre und Stille genießen, wie es ein Fluss bietet?

Clockwise from top left: *The wood interior is glazed a warm parchment yellow; the wood-burning stove keeps the snug interior warm and dry; the boat has a few non-essentials, including this baby upright piano; a child's wood and canvas model square-rigger and a watery painting are subtle reminders of the interior's location.*

Du haut à gauche, dans le sens des aiguilles d'une montre: *A l'intérieur, toutes les boiseries sont vernies dans un jaune parchemin chaleureux; le poêle à bois garde l'intérieur douillet au chaud et au sec; le bateau abrite quelques éléments accessoires tels que ce mini-piano droit;*

la maquette naïve d'un trois-mâts et la marine accrochée au mur rappellent discrètement que l'on se trouve sur un bateau.

Im Uhrzeigersinn von links oben: *Das für den Innenbereich verwendete Holz wurde in einem sanften Pergamentgelb lackiert; der holzbefeuerte Herd sorgt dafür, dass es im Innern kuschelig warm und trocken ist; zur Bootsausstattung gehört auch einiges, das nicht »lebensnotwendig« ist – wie dieser Stutzflügel; ein voll getakeltes Spielzeugschiff aus Holz und Leinwand sowie ein Seestück an der Wand erinnern an das eigentliche Umfeld.*

In this corner of the living room, a wall is covered in soft metal sheeting; velvet swag curtains and a Persian carpet prevent draughts from coming down from the wheelhouse above; the furniture is a comfortable mix of a French gilt sofa, an English mahogany writing desk and a lighthouse lamp used as a coffee table.

Dans ce coin du salon, un mur est tapissé de feuilles de métal mou. Les rideaux en velours froncé et le tapis persan empêchent les courants d'air de filtrer depuis la timonerie située plus haut. Le mobilier est composé d'un assortiment nonchalant. un canapé français en bois

doré, un secrétaire anglais en acajou et une lampe de phare faisant office de table basse.

Die Wand dieser Wohnzimmerecke ist mit Metall verschalt und mit üppigen Samtvorhängen und einem persischen Teppich ausgestattet, die den Zug aus dem darüber liegenden Ruderhaus abfangen. Das Mobiliar ist ein lässiger Mix aus Französisch (das vergoldete Sofa), Englisch (der Schreibtisch aus Mahagoni) und Maritimem (ein Leuchtturm-Scheinwerfer dient als Beistelltisch).

The master bedroom is built into the stern of the vessel and apart from the restricted headroom it is as luxuriously fitted out as any land-bound bedroom. Here shelving and tables are built in, providing lots of room for books, lights and other bedtime needs. Two antique carved oak pillars were used in the construction of the bed.

La chambre des maîtres est nichée sous la poupe et, même si le plafond est bas, elle est aussi luxueusement aménagée que n'importe quelle chambre de la terre ferme. Sur un bateau, le plus grand défi est sans doute l'espace de rangement. Ici, étagères et tables de nuit sont encastrées pour laisser le plus de place possible aux livres, aux lampes et à tout ce dont on peut avoir besoin à son chevet. Deux anciennes colonnes en chêne sculpté ont été utilisées pour construire le lit.

Das große Schlafzimmer ist in das Bootsheck eingebaut. Die niedrige Höhe mag zwar etwas einschränkend wirken, aber es verfügt über allen Luxus, den man auch an Land hat. Hier wurden Regale und Tische eingebaut, um ausreichend Platz für Bücher, Lichtquellen und andere Dinge zu bieten. Für die Bettkonstruktion dienten zwei alte geschnitzte Eichensäulen.

Clockwise from top left: *The main bathroom is well-organised, with an elegant Victorian marble and mahogany washbasin and heated towel rail adding a sense of luxury; an overhead hatch lets in enough light; the bath has a border of highly varnished teak; in the master bedroom, a sunken bath complete with bathing buckets.*

Du haut à gauche, dans le sens des aiguilles d'une montre: *La salle de bains principale est bien conçue, avec un élégant lavabo victorien en marbre et acajou et, comble du luxe, un porte-serviettes chauffant; une écoutille laisse passer suffisamment de lumière; la baignoire a un rebord en teck généreusement verni; dans la chambre des maîtres, une baignoire enchâssée dans le sol avec des seaux de bain.*

Im Uhrzeigersinn von links oben: *Das große, gut durchorganisierte Bad ist trotzdem auch luxuriös, dank des viktorianischen Waschbeckens aus Marmor und Mahagoni und des beheizbaren Handtuchhalters; eine Luke sorgt für ausreichendes Licht; die Einfassung im Bad besteht aus lackiertem Teak; das große Schlafzimmer verfügt über eine in den Boden eingelassene Badewanne, worauf kleine Badezuber stehen.*

Il y a trois ans, Shaun Clarkson et Paul Brewster décidèrent qu'ils en avaient assez de la banlieue et voulaient une ambiance «urbaine». Ils ont trouvé leur bonheur au premier étage d'un ancien atelier d'imprimerie victorien au cœur de Shoreditch, à l'est de Londres. Shaun Clarkson explique: «On voulait un vrai espace de travail et de vie, un endroit où on se sentirait efficaces sans stress». L'idée maîtresse était de garder l'appartement simple et dépouillé, avec une séparation physique et psychologique bien définie entre le bureau alcôve de Shaun et le vaste espace de séjour. Shaun, sculpteur et décorateur, a un faible pour le flamboyant et le décoratif, Paul, qui possède une entreprise de textiles de mode, impose plus de retenue. Néanmoins, quelques touches de frivolités, de couleurs et d'ornements se sont glissées ici et là, notamment l'énorme lustre en cristal qui domine la cuisine.

Shaun Clarkson & Paul Brewster

Three years ago, Shaun Clarkson and Paul Brewster decided they wanted "an urban, not suburban vibe" and found just that on the first floor of this Victorian former printing workshop in the heart of Shoreditch in East London. Shaun explains: "We wanted a real live and work space, a place to live in efficiently and be stress-free." Keeping it simple and uncluttered was the key, with a clear physical and psychological divide between Shaun's alcove office and the open-plan living area. While Shaun, a sculptor and interior designer, has tastes which veer towards the flamboyant and decorative, Paul, who owns a fashion textile business, imposes a more restrained influence. However, touches of frivolity, colour and decorative detail have been allowed to creep in, noticeably the enormous crystal chandelier which dominates the kitchen.

Vor drei Jahren beschlossen Shaun Clarkson und Paul Brewster, ihrem Leben einen »urbanen und keinen suburbanen« Touch zu geben. Diesen fanden sie im ersten Stock einer ehemaligen viktorianischen Druckereiwerkstatt in Shoreditch im Osten Londons. Shaun Clarkson erklärt, dass sie »nach einer authentischen, realistischen Arbeitsatmosphäre« gesucht hätten, in der man »effizient und stressfrei leben kann«. Wichtig waren Einfachheit und Schlichtheit – nichts sollte überladen sein oder vollgestopft wirken – und eine klare physische und psychologische Trennung zwischen Shaun Clarksons Alkoven-Büro und dem als Großraum konzipierten Wohnbereich herrschen. Shaun Clarkson, Bildhauer und Innenarchitekt, hat eine Vorliebe für Extravagantes und Dekoratives. Paul Brewster hingegen, dem ein Unternehmen für Modestoffe gehört, gibt einen etwas zurückhaltenderen Ton vor. Doch hier und da darf in den Details das Frivole, Bunte und Dekorative hervortreten, zum Beispiel in dem riesigen Kristalllüster, der die Küche beherrscht.

First page: The kitchen, which also acts as a transitional space between the open-plan living room and private bedroom and bathroom areas of the flat, is painted an exuberant lilac.
Above: The elegant curves of a 1960s chrome and glass floor lamp define the informal dining and meeting area. Two prototype concrete lamps by Babylon Design stand on the metal-framed windowsill.

Première page: La cuisine fait le lien entre la salle de séjour d'un côté, et la chambre et la salle de bains de l'autre.
Ci-dessus: La courbe élégante d'un lampadaire en chrome et en verre

des années 1960 définit l'espace où l'on dîne et reçoit. Sur le rebord de la fenêtre, deux prototypes de lampes en béton de Babylon Design.

Eingangsseite: Die Küche ist gleichzeitig Übergang zwischen dem als Großraum angelegten Wohnzimmer und dem privaten Bereich von Schlaf- und Badezimmer.
Oben: Aus den 1960er Jahren stammt diese Stehlampe aus Chrom und Glas. Im Empfangs- und Essbereich setzen ihre eleganten Kurven Akzente. Auf der in Metall gefassten Fensterbank stehen die Prototypen von zwei Lampen aus Beton von Babylon Design.

London Interiors   Shaun Clarkson & Paul Brewster

Paul and Shaun plan to insert a sunken seating area in the future – at present the vast white space is dominated by a purple velvet sofa, one of Shaun's original designs for a nightclub.

Paul et Shaun projettent de créer un coin salon en cuvette dans cette partie de l'appartement, à présent occupée par un canapé en velours violet, que Shaun avait dessiné à l'origine pour un night-club.

Ein Zukunftsprojekt von Paul Brewster und Shaun Clarkson ist ein versenkbarer Sitzbereich. Im Moment wird der große weiße Raum noch von einem Sofa mit lilafarbenem Samtbezug bestimmt – eines von mehreren Originalen, die Shaun Clarkson für einen Nachtclub entworfen hat.

Wood doors opening out onto the first-floor delivery platform are painted an unexpected shade of pink. A silver-leafed screen wall prevents a direct view into the bedroom beyond and reflects light back into the kitchen.

Détail inattendu: les portes en bois qui s'ouvrent sur le monte-charge sont peintes en rose. Un paravent traité à la feuille d'argent cache la chambre qui se trouve juste derrière et réfléchit la lumière dans la cuisine.

Holztüren öffnen sich zu einer Anlieferungsrampe im ersten Stock. Überraschend ist ihr Farbanstrich in Pink. Eine mit Blattsilber bezogene Trennwand versperrt den Blick auf das dahinter liegende Schlafzimmer und wirft das Licht zurück in die Küche.

London Interiors   Shaun Clarkson & Paul Brewster

Clockwise from top left: *A sturdy 1960s food processor and other functional pieces of kitchen equipment surround a decorative Chinese altar; in the bedroom, Shaun's gilt and glass mosaic Hoover was made 1989; in the kitchen, the Indian painted-wood panels are two of seven; the white retro-looking side tables were designed by Shaun.*

Du haut à gauche, dans le sens des aiguilles d'une montre: *un robuste mixeur des années 1960 et d'autres appareils ménagers entourent un autel chinois; dans la chambre à coucher, un aspirateur doré en mosaïque de verre créé par Shaun en 1989; les deux panneaux in-*

diens en bois peint font partie d'une série de sept; Shaun a dessiné les deux petites tables latérales «rétros».

Im Uhrzeigersinn von links oben: *Eine robuste Küchenmaschine aus den 1960er Jahren und weitere Küchenutensilien sind um einen chinesischen Altar gruppiert; Shaun Clarkson schuf 1989 den Mosaik-Staubsauger aus Glas und Gold; sieben aus Indien stammende bemalte Holzpaneele, hier zwei in der Küche, wurden bei einem Trödler für einen Apfel und ein Ei erworben; die weißen Beistelltischchen mit Retrocharme sind ein Entwurf von Shaun Clarkson.*

Above: Shaun has his small but perfectly planned office in a light-filled alcove off the main living space.
Right: A floor-to-ceiling velvet padded screen wall also serves as a deluxe headboard. The Indian theme also continues in the bedroom, with gold-embroidered cushions and brass vases that have been converted into lamps.

Ci-dessus: Shaun s'est aménagé un bureau minuscule mais parfaitement agencé dans une alcôve inondée de lumière qui jouxte le grand séjour.
A droite: L'écran en velours capitonné qui va du sol au plafond fait aussi office de tête de lit. Le thème indien se poursuit dans la chambre avec des coussins brodés d'or et des vases en laiton montés en lampes de chevet.

Oben: Shauns Büro ist klein, aber perfekt durchgeplant. Es liegt in einem lichtdurchfluteten Alkoven über dem Wohnbereich.
Rechts: Vom Boden bis zur Decke reicht diese samtbezogene Trennwand, die gleichzeitig als luxuriöse Kopfstütze dient. Im Schlafzimmer setzt sich das Thema Indien in der Dekoration fort: mit goldbestickten Kissen und Messingvasen, die zu Lampen umfunktioniert wurden.

London Interiors   Shaun Clarkson & Paul Brewster

Il y a six ans, cette maison du début du 18ᵉ siècle au nord de Londres
était un dédale de pièces aux cloisons en placoplâtre et parées de
chintz et d'appliques en cuivre. Les propriétaires actuels lui ont rendu
sa dignité, tout en y ajoutant leur propre vision esthétique. La maison
ne comporte qu'une pièce par étage, avec de petites chambres tapissées de lambris typiques de l'époque à laquelle elle a été construite.
«Avant de venir vivre ici», expliquent les propriétaires, «nous ache-
tions beaucoup de meubles des années 1930 et 1940. A présent, nous
recherchons surtout des pièces des années 1740, contemporaines de la
maison, les seules qui aient les proportions adaptées». Toutefois, leur
vaste collection d'art comprend aussi bien des photographies et des tableaux de l'ère victorienne que des œuvres contemporaines. Ils possè-
dent de nombreuses pièces des Young British Artists, achetées avant
que les galeries et Charles Saatchi ne s'intéressent à ce courant, à une
époque où ces jeunes artistes n'avaient d'autre choix que de présenter
leur travail dans des squats délabrés et des entrepôts.

The Collectors

Six years ago, this early 18th-century north London town house was
a warren of plaster-boarded rooms, decked out in chintz and brass
wall light fittings. The present owners have since restored the
house's integral Georgian dignity, while adding their own strong
aesthetic vision. It is a wide building, but only one room deep, with
small-scale panelled rooms that are typical of the period in which it
was built. The owner explains: "Before we lived here, we bought a
lot of 1930s and 1940s furniture, but now we buy early English
pieces from around the 1740s, the same period as the house, otherwise it's hard to find proportions that look right." However, their
extensive art collection spans Victorian photography and painting
to contemporary works. Many pieces are by Young British Artists,
bought before the galleries and Charles Saatchi got involved, a
time when young artists had no choice but to show their work in
derelict buildings and warehouses.

Vor sechs Jahren war dieses aus dem frühen 18. Jahrhundert stammende »town house« im Norden Londons noch eine Mischung aus
Labyrinth und Kaninchenbau. Die Wände waren aus Gipskarton, und
in den Räumen hatten Chintz und Messingleuchten das Sagen. Die
jetzigen Inhaber haben dem Haus seine georgianische Würde zurück-
gegeben und ihm trotzdem ihre persönliche ästhetische Note verliehen. Das Haus ist zwar breit, aber nur einen Raum tief und besitzt
die für diese Zeit typischen, kleinen getäfelten Zimmer. »Vor unserem
Einzug hatten wir viele Möbel aus den 1930er und 1940er Jahren erworben«, erklärt der Hausherr. »Jetzt kaufen wir allerdings Stücke
aus frühenglischer Zeit um 1740, der Epoche, der dieses Haus ent-
stammt. Sonst wird es schwierig, Proportionen zu finden, die auch
wirklich zu dem Haus passen.« Doch die umfangreiche Kunstsamm-
lung reicht von der viktorianischen Zeit bis heute und deckt Fotografie
sowie Malerei ab. Viele Arbeiten stammen von Young British Artists
und wurden gekauft, bevor Galerien und Charles Saatchi tätig wurden, und die Künstler noch ihre Arbeiten in abbruchreifen Häusern
und Lagerräumen zeigten.

Previous pages: In the entrance hall, a Sarah Lucas photograph above a goblet by American artist Thomas Lanigan-Schmidt. The display plinth contains Martin Creed's "screwed-up ball of paper".
Right: In the smaller reception room, Andy Goldsworthy's "balanced winstone" stands next to a 1738 giltwood chair designed by William Kent. Above hangs an Art Deco oil-on-board portrait by Gerda Wegener.
Below: In the reception room, Andy Goldsworthy's "fired earth", a ring of baked stones, surrounds a structural column. In the background, an 18th-century Hepplewhite sofa.

Double page précédente: Dans l'entrée, une photographie de Sarah Lucas est accrochée au-dessus d'un calice de l'Américain Thomas Lanigan-Schmidt. Dans la vitrine, une «boule de papier froissée», de Martin Creed.
A droite: Dans la petite réception, la «Pierre en équilibre», d'Andy Goldsworthy est placée près d'un fauteuil en bois doré de William Kent, datant de 1738. Au-dessus, un portrait Art Déco à l'huile sur bois de Gerda Wegener.
Ci-dessous: Dans la grande réception, un cercle de pierres cuites, «Terre calcinée», d'Andy Goldsworthy, entoure une colonne portante. A l'arrière-fond, un canapé Hepplewhite du 18ᵉ siècle.

Vorhergehende Doppelseite: Im Eingangsbereich hängt eine Fotografie von Sarah Lucas über einem Trinkbecher des amerikanischen Künstlers Thomas Lanigan-Schmidt. Im Schaukasten befindet sich »screwed-up ball of paper« von Martin Creed.
Rechts: Im kleineren Salon steht Andy Goldsworthys »balanced winstone« neben einem vergoldeten Holzstuhl aus dem Jahr 1738, einem Entwurf von William Kent. Darüber hängt ein Art-Deco-Porträt in Öl auf Pappe von Gerda Wegener.
Unten: Im Empfangsraum umzieht ein Ring von gebrannten Steinen – »fired earth« von Andy Goldsworthy – einen Stützpfeiler. Das Hepplewhite-Sofa vor der Wand stammt aus dem 18. Jahrhundert.

Above: Sitting on a 1940s Hermès rocking chair is "fuck-face" by Jake and Dinos Chapman. The leaf box sculpture is by Andy Goldsworthy. A painting by Sir George Frampton, flanked by old Sheffield plate candlesticks, hangs above the mantelpiece. Late Victorian drawings by Herbert Draper hang to the left and right of the fireplace.
Right: In the smaller reception room, the 1780s fireplace is gradually being restored. Above is a painting by Zebedee Jones as well as two "drowning faces" by Angus Fairhurst.

Ci-dessus: Assis sur un fauteuil à bascule Hermès des années 1940, «Fuck-face» de Jake et Dinos Chapman. La sculpture de boîte en feuilles est d'Andy Goldsworthy. Un tableau de sir George Frampton est flanqué de paires de bougeoirs anciens Sheffield posés sur le manteau de cheminée. Des dessins d'Herbert Draper datant de la fin de l'ère victorienne sont accrochés à gauche et à droite de la cheminée.
A droite: Dans la petite réception, la cheminée datant des années 1780 est en cours de restauration . Au-dessus, un tableau de Zebedee Jones et deux «visages sombrants» d'Angus Fairhurst.

Oben: Auf einem Hermès-Schaukelstuhl aus den 1940er Jahren thront ein »fuck-face« von Jake und Dinos Chapman. Die »leaf box«-Skulptur stammt von Andy Goldsworthy. Auf dem Kaminsims rahmen alte Kerzenleuchter aus Sheffield-Silber ein Gemälde von Sir George Frampton. Zeichnungen von Herbert Draper aus spätviktorianischer Zeit hängen zu beiden Seiten des Kamins.
Rechts: Im kleineren Empfangszimmer wird der aus dem Jahr 1780 stammende Kamin Stück für Stück restauriert. Darüber hängt ein Bild von Zebedee Jones und zwei »drowning faces« von Angus Fairhurst.

Above: Fine cotton lawn drapes hang over the crib in the child's bedroom, while above a wicker box of clothes and a pair of stuffed rabbits on the bed is a drawing by Tracey Emin. One of the owners, who is an artist, painted the walls throughout the house.
Facing page: One of their four Burmese cats sprawls on a Northumbrian quilt. Above is a painting by Zebedee Jones, while to the left a silk 19th-century Central Asian "ikat" textile can be seen.

Ci-dessus: Dans la chambre d'enfant, un fin voile de coton recouvre le berceau. Au-dessus du panier en osier et de deux lapins en peluche posés sur le lit, un dessin de Tracey Emin. L'un des propriétaires, également artiste, a peint tous les murs de la maison.
Page de droite: l'un des quatre chats burmese, voluptueusement étendu sur une couette de Northumbria. Au mur, un tableau de Zebedee Jones. Sur la gauche, on aperçoit un ikat d'Asie centrale datant du 19ᵉ siècle.

Oben: Die Vorhänge der Wiege im Kinderzimmer sind aus Batist. Auf dem Bett liegen ein Weidenkörbchen und zwei Plüschkaninchen. Darüber hängt eine Zeichnung von Tracey Emin. Einer der beiden Bewohner – selbst Künstler – hat im ganzen Haus die Wände bemalt.
Rechte Seite: Eine der vier Burmakatzen hat es sich auf einem Quilt aus Northumbria gemütlich gemacht. Über ihr hängt ein Bild von Zebedee Jones. Links daneben sieht man einen zentralasiatischen seidenen Ikat aus dem 19. Jahrhundert.

Below: A large copper catering bowl has been used to create a sink on a glass plinth in the main bathroom, while a Baccarat glass, used to hold toothbrushes, adds another light-reflective element.

Ci-dessous: Dans la salle de bains principale, le lavabo est une grande coupe en cuivre posée sur un pied en verre. Le verre en cristal de Baccarat dans lequel sont rangées les brosses à dents offre une autre surface réfléchissante.

Unten: Eine große Schüssel aus Kupfer, wie sie Caterer verwenden, wurde als Waschschüssel zweckentfremdet und steht im großen Badezimmer auf einem Glaspodest. Das Baccarat-Glas für die Zahnbürsten reflektiert ebenfalls das Licht.

Facing page: The owner used shellac-glazed oil paint in cerulean blue for the walls in the main bathroom. The cupboards have been gold-leafed. Copper sheeting surrounds the bath and is used on the floor, too, creating a light-reflecting surface.
Above: A long corridor and second bathroom were added to the back section of the house as the original building was wide, but only one room deep. In this bathroom, mosaic tiles have a modern feel and echo the graphic lines of the room. The two ceramic pots are from Habitat.

Page de gauche: Les propriétaires ont peint les murs de la salle de bains principale en bleu céruléen à l'huile vernis à la gomme-laque. Les placards sont dorés à la feuille. Les feuilles de cuivre sur la baignoire et le sol créent des surfaces réfléchissantes.
Ci-dessus: Un long couloir et une seconde salle de bains ont été ajoutés à l'arrière de la maison, le bâtiment étant vaste mais trop peu profond. Les carreaux de mosaïque ont une allure moderne en harmonie avec les lignes géométriques de la pièce. Les deux pots en céramique viennent de chez Habitat.

Linke Seite: Ölfarbe mit Schellackfinish in Nachtblau bedeckt die Wände im großen Badezimmer. Die Schränke wurden mit Blattgold überzogen. Die Badewanne ist mit Kupferplatten eingefaßt, die auch auf dem Boden verlegt sind und eine lichtreflektierende Oberfläche schaffen.
Oben: An der rückwärtigen Seite des Hauses wurden ein langer Korridor und ein zweites Badezimmer angebaut, denn die ursprüngliche Bausubstanz war zwar breit, aber nur zimmertief. Mosaikfliesen verleihen diesem Badezimmer einen modernen Touch und greifen die grafischen Linien des Raums auf. Die beiden Keramikdosen stammen von Habitat.

Assise sur un canapé tapissé de Lycra noir et d'applications en soie rose, Carolyn Corben cherche les mots qui décriront au mieux son appartement de Clapham. «Une sorte d'éclectisme décoratif mais plutôt minimal, en somme». Si, à première vue, son «minimalisme» ne saute pas au yeux, on se rend compte au bout d'un moment qu'elle dit vrai. Il y a peu de meubles ou de bibelots et le système de rangement est extrêmement bien organisé. «J'ai évité d'avoir trop de surfaces horizontales afin de ne pas être tentée d'y déposer tout un fouillis». En revanche, le moindre centimètre carré de mur et de plafond est décoré. On y trouve des écritures car elle aime «la qualité décorative des mots», des cartes topographiques qui lui rappellent la peau, «les routes sont comme des veines et des artères», et des photocopies couleur agrandies de tableaux de maître qui créent un effet d'opulence. «Elles sont très New RenaisCAnce.», affirme-t-elle en faisant allusion à la société de création unique en son genre qu'elle a créée avec son ancien camarade du Royal College of Art, Harvey Bertram-Brown.

Carolyn Corben

Sitting on a black lycra and silk rose appliqué sofa, Carolyn Corben searches for words to describe her Clapham flat: "It's sort of decorative eclecticism, but actually quite minimal," she says. While first impressions don't exactly shout Minimal, on closer inspection she's right; there isn't much in the way of furniture or knick-knacks, and the storage is extremely well-organised. "I am naturally quite messy, so I avoided having lots of horizontal surfaces, which I would only end up covering in clutter." Instead, she has covered every inch of the walls and ceilings with decoration: with lettering because she "loves the decorative quality of words"; with Ordnance Survey maps because they remind her of skin ("the roads are veins and arteries"); and with enlarged colour photocopies of classical paintings, which are "very New RenaisCAnce," she says, referring to the unique multifaceted creative company she formed with fellow ex-Royal College of Art student Harvey Bertram-Brown.

Auf ihrem schwarzem Lycrasofa mit Applikationen aus rosafarbener Seide sitzend sucht Carolyn Corben nach Worten, die ihre Wohnung in Clapham beschreiben würden: »eine Art dekorativer Eklektizismus, aber eigentlich sehr minimal«, sagt sie. Der erste Eindruck ist zwar kaum minimalistisch, aber auf den zweiten Blick hat sie durchaus Recht: Es gibt wenig Möbel oder Schnickschnack, und der Stauraum ist ausgesprochen gut organisiert. »Ich bin von Natur aus sehr unordentlich. Deswegen vermeide ich zu viele horizontale Flächen. Die würde ich nämlich nur vollstellen.« Stattdessen hat sie jeden Zentimeter der Wände und Decken dekoriert: mit Schriften, weil sie »die dekorative Qualität der Worte« liebt; mit Landvermessungskarten, weil diese sie an Haut erinnern (die Straßen sind Venen und Arterien). Und mit Farbfotovergrößerungen klassischer Gemälde, weil sie »typisch für New RenaisCAnce sind, opulent, aber trotzdem einfach herzustellen«, sagt sie und bezieht sich dabei auf die außergewöhnliche Kreativ-Company, die sie mit Harvey Bertram-Brown, ihrem früheren Kommilitonen am Royal College of Art, gegründet hat.

Previous page: The walls in the bedroom are covered in blown-up colour photocopies; this is "Gabrielle d'Estrées and one of her sisters", which is attributed to the school of Fontainebleau (the original hangs in the Louvre).
Right: Corben designed the table, which incorporates a large map of central London protected by glass in a metal frame.
Below: The practicality of restaurant kitchen design inspired Corben to use stainless steel, but she also wanted the work area to look into the rest of the room. The solution was biomorphic work surfaces over metal-faced units.

Page précédente: Les murs de la chambre sont tapissés de photocopies couleur agrandies. Ici, «Gabrielle d'Estrées et l'une de ses sœurs», attribué à l'école de Fontainebleau. L'original est au Louvre.
A droite: Corben a dessiné la table dont le plateau est constitué d'une grande carte du centre de Londres sous verre.
Ci-dessous: Séduite par le côté pratique des cuisines de restaurant, Corben a opté pour de l'acier inoxydable mais voulait que son plan de travail soit harmonisé avec le reste de la pièce. Sa solution personnelle: un comptoir biomorphique posé sur des modules recouverts de feuilles de métal.

Vorhergehende Seite: Die Wände im Schlafzimmer bedecken vergrößerte Fotokopien, darunter »Gabrielle d'Estrées und eine ihrer Schwestern«; das Original wird der Schule von Fontainebleau zugeschrieben und hängt im Louvre.
Rechts: Den Tisch mit einer riesigen Karte der Londoner Innenstadt, die durch Glas geschützt wird, hat Carolyn Corben selbst entworfen.
Unten: Die Funktionalität von Restaurantküchen inspirierte Carolyn Corben zur Verwendung von rostfreiem Stahl. Da sie wollte, dass der Arbeitsbereich in den Rest des Raumes übergeht, entwarf sie biomorphe Arbeitsflächen auf metallverkleideten Elementen.

Above: Corben wanted words, but couldn't decide which ones until she saw Douglas Gordon's Turner Prize exhibition at The Tate Gallery and his ambiguous "Untitled text for somewhere other than here". Corben gave it a home other than The Tate by pasting cut-outs of letters in thin card onto the walls and applying a layer of gold paint to create a subtle relief.
Right: Corben practises Nichiren Daishonin Buddhism for 90 minutes a day; the sheet of gold paper provides the only plain image to focus on in the flat.

Ci-dessus: Corben voulait des mots mais n'arrivait pas à décider lesquels jusqu'à ce qu'elle voit l'exposition Turner Prize de Douglas Gordon à la Tate Gallery et son ambigu «Texte sans titre pour mettre ailleurs qu'ici». Corben l'a donc accueilli ailleurs qu'à la Tate en collant des lettres découpées dans du bristol sur les murs puis en les recouvrant d'une couche de peinture pour créer un subtil effet de relief.
A droite: Corben pratique les rites du bouddhisme Nichiren Daishonin une heure et demie par jour. La feuille de papier doré accrochée au mur, seule surface vide de tout l'appartement, lui sert à se concentrer pendant sa méditation.

Oben: Carolyn Corben wollte Worte, aber welche, das wusste sie erst, nachdem sie Douglas Gordons Arbeit »Untitled text for somewhere other than here« bei der Turner-Prize-Ausstellung in der Tate Gallery gesehen hatte. Sie gab dem Werk außerhalb der Tate Gallery ein Zuhause. Lettern wurden ausgeschnitten, auf dünne Pappe montiert, auf den Wänden verklebt und dann mit einer dünnen Schicht Gold überzogen, um ein Reliefmuster zu erzielen.
Rechts: Eineinhalb Stunden täglich dauert Corbens Religionsausübung (Nishiren Daishonin Buddhismus). Das Blatt Goldpapier ist die einzige plane Oberfläche, auf die man sich konzentrieren kann.

Smithfields Market, London EC1

Joseph Corré et Serena Rees sont partenaires en affaires comme dans la vie, gérant leurs entreprises florissantes depuis leur Q.G. de Clerkenwell, à deux pas de leur appartement dans une ancienne usine d'ascenseurs. Propriétaires d'Agent Provocateur, la seule grande boutique de lingerie sexy digne de ce nom en Grande-Bretagne, et représentants britanniques d'Edra, la compagnie italienne de mobilier, leur intérieur reflète admirablement ce double jeu. Il s'agit essentiellement d'une grande pièce avec une chambre à coucher cachée derrière des rideaux. «Qùand on a aménagé, on a simplement déposé tout ce qu'on possédait au hasard. Puis, tout est resté plus ou moins comme ça», explique Serena. Rees, Corré et leur fille Cora emménageront bientôt dans un nouvel appartement situé au-dessus de leur showroom. Au rez-de-chaussée, vendant des sous-vêtements diaboliques et des meubles fabuleux, des coquettes trottinent sur le parquet du 18e siècle en causant des dommages irréparables avec leurs talons aiguilles.

Joseph Corré & Serena Rees

Joseph Corré and Serena Rees are partners in both work and life, running their expanding business from headquarters in Clerkenwell, a short distance from their home in an old lift factory. As owners of Agent Provocateur, London's only seriously sexy lingerie emporium, and UK agents for Edra, the Italian furniture company, their home perfectly reflects their joint creative vision. Essentially one large room with a partitioned-off bedroom, Serena explains simply: "What we already owned was just thrown into the space. That's how it ended up looking, really." Rees, Corré and their daughter Cora will soon be moving into the house above the showroom. Downstairs, selling an alluring mix of devilish undies and fabulous furniture, saucy assistants teeter on their stilettos, doing untold damage to the Georgian wood floors.

Joseph Corré und Serena Rees sind Geschäfts- und Lebenspartner. Ihr expandierendes Unternehmen leiten sie vom Stammhaus in Clerkenwell aus, nicht weit entfernt von ihrem Zuhause in einer ehemaligen Fahrstuhlfabrik. Corré und Rees sind Inhaber von Agent Provocateur, Londons einzigem Dessous-Geschäft, das wirklich sexy ist; außerdem haben sie die englische Generalvertretung für den italienischen Möbelfabrikanten Edra. Diese gemeinsame kreative Vision spiegelt sich in ihrem Zuhause wider, das eigentlich nur aus einem riesigen Raum mit einem abgetrennten Schlafzimmer besteht. »Wir haben einfach alle unsere Sachen auf diese riesige Fläche gekippt. Und so ist es dann auch geblieben«, erklärt Serena Rees. Bald werden Rees, Corré und ihr Töchterchen Cora umziehen in das Haus, in dem sich ihr Showroom befindet. Dort verkaufen sie eine faszinierende Mischung aus heißen Dessous und hinreißenden Möbeln. Kesse Assistentinnen stöckeln auf Stilettoabsätzen über den aus georgianischer Zeit stammenden Holzfußboden und hinterlassen unübersehbare Spuren.

Previous page: In their showroom, Serena Rees reclines against a black and white photograph by Ellen von Unwerth taken for iD Magazine. Joseph Corré sits on an Edra chair.
Above: Two Edra "Square" armchairs covered in hi-speed fabric, a tricot weave that was originally developed for bobsled suits.

Page précédente: Dans le showroom, Serena Rees est adossée à une photographie en noir et blanc d'Ellen von Unwerth, prise pour le magazine iD. Joseph Corré est assis dans un fauteuil d'Edra.
Ci-dessus: Les deux fauteuils « Square » d'Edra sont habillés d'un revêtement élaboré pour les tenues de pilotes de bobsleigh.

Vorhergehende Seite: im Showroom. Hinter Serena Rees hängt ein Schwarzweißfoto von Ellen von Unwerth, aufgenommen für das Magazin iD. Joseph Corré sitzt auf einem »Square«-Sessel von Edra.
Oben: Die beiden Sessel von Edra sind mit einem speziellen Bezug versehen, der für Anzüge von Bobfahrern entwickelt wurde.

Above the sofa version of the "Square" chair hang two paintings by John Willie which were painted as covers for the cult 1950s magazine Bizarre.

Au-dessus de la version canapé du fauteuil «Square» sont suspendues deux œuvres de John Willie, peintes au cours des années 1950 pour la couverture du magazine culte Bizarre.

Über der Sofa-Version des »Square«-Sessels von Edra hängen zwei Werke von John Willie, die er in den 1950ern als Covermotive für das Kultmagazin Bizarre malte.

Above: *The gilt-framed collage of Great Train Robber Ronnie Biggs is part of Joseph's collection of Sex Pistols memorabilia. The curtains to the left are Vivienne Westwood fabric. Westwood is Joseph's mother from her relationship with Malcolm McLaren.*
Right: *Their two toasters were brought together from the days before they became a couple, but as Serena sensibly says: "You can never have enough slots for toast, can you?"*

Ci-dessus: *Dans son cadre doré, le collage de The Great Train Robber Ronnie Bigs fait partie de la collection de Joseph d'objets liés aux Sex Pistols. Les rideaux sont cousus dans un tissu de Westwood. Joseph est le fils de Vivienne Westwood et de Malcom McLaren.*
A droite: *Serena et Joseph ont acheté ensemble leur toasters à l'époque où ils ne formaient pas encore un couple mais, comme dit Serena, «on a toujours besoin de faire griller plusieurs toasts simulta-nément, non?»*

Oben: *In Gold gerahmt ist die Collage des Posträubers Ronnie Biggs – sie ist Teil von Joseph Corrés Sammlung von Erinnerungsstücken an die Sex Pistols. Die Vorhänge zur Linken entwarf Vivienne Westwood, die Mutter von Joseph Corré; sein Vater ist Malcolm McLaren.*
Rechts: *Die beiden Toaster stammen noch aus den Singlezeiten der Partner. »Aber«, meint Serena Rees sehr vernünftig, »Toaster kann man doch nie genug haben, oder?«*

London Interiors   Joseph Corré & Serena Rees

Clockwise from top left: *Some of Serena's Agent Provocateur undies are kept in a little trunk; on the kitchen table, glass millinery beads, ceramic chickens and an Alessi Moo Moo parmesan cheese container; divinely indulgent turquoise tulle bra, knickers and suspender belt; a kitsch Eiffel tower and framed pictures.*

Du haut à gauche, dans le sens des aiguilles d'une montre: *Serena conserve certains de ses sous-vêtements d'Agent Provocateur dans un petit coffre; sur la table de la cuisine, des épingles à chapeaux de verre, des coqs en céramique et une boîte à parmesan d'Alessi baptisée Moo Moo; un soutien-gorge, un slip et un porte-jarretelles en tulle turquoise délicieusement coquins; une tour Eiffel kitsch et des cadres de photos.*

Im Uhrzeigersinn von oben links: *Einen Teil ihrer Dessous von Agent Provocateur bewahrt Serena Rees in einem Köfferchen auf; auf dem Küchentisch liegen gläserne Hutnadeln neben Keramikhähnen und der Parmesandose Moo Moo von Alessi; göttliche Dessous: BH, Höschen und Strapse aus türkisfarbenem Tüll; ein kitschiger Eiffelturm und gerahmte Fotos.*

London Interiors Joseph Corré & Serena Rees

The bedroom feels intimate and boudoir-like. The French bed was bought at auction and the headboard was covered in Westwood's "Boulle" print denim, as was the chair. Not afraid of a bit of tat, the chinoiserie-style table is "nothing special", while on it stands a bizarrely kitsch lamp bought by Serena in a Seattle junk shop.

La chambre à coucher a l'atmosphère intime d'un boudoir. Le lit français a été acheté dans une vente aux enchères. La tête de lit est tapissée d'un tissu Westwood, «Boulle», en jean imprimé, tout comme le fauteuil. Les propriétaires ne craignant pas la camelote, la table en chinoiserie est de la «bricole». Dessus, une lampe étrangement kitsch achetée par Serena chez un brocanteur de Seattle.

Im Schlafzimmer fühlt man sich geborgen wie in einem Boudoir. Das französische Bett wurde auf einer Auktion erstanden. Kopfteil und Stuhl sind mit Vivienne Westwoods Stoff »Boulle« aus bedrucktem Denim bezogen. Rees und Corré fürchten sich vor Trödel nicht: Der Chinoiserie-Tisch ist »nichts Besonderes«, auf ihm thront eine bizarre Kitschlampe, die Serena Rees bei einem Trödler in Seattle gekauft hat.

Le titre officiel de Dave Courtney, «conseiller en sécurité», peut paraître anodin, mais c'est surtout en tant que porte-parole de la pègre londonienne qu'il est connu. «Tout le monde nourrit des idées préconçues à mon égard», explique-t-il en riant. «Dans les rangs de la police, le bruit court même que je fais fortifier ma maison, comme si je fomentais une opération à la Waco, ou quelque chose du genre!». Pour un homme qui se délecte manifestement de l'ambiguïté de son rôle, il semble étonnamment normal. Sa maison est un véritable camp de base pour une armée d'amis, de parents et d'employés qui vont et viennent. Même les équipes de télévision et les journalistes de passage sont accueillis chaleureusement par sa femme Jennifer, alias Club MC Jenny Bean, qui fait passer des assiettes de sandwichs au bacon et des tasses de thé à tous les nouveaux arrivants. Fier de sa demeure, Courtney précise qu'il a surtout été influencé par la cour du roi Arthur. « L'image de la table ronde était toujours dans ma tête.» Pour lui, tout Anglais digne de ce nom doit faire de sa maison un château.

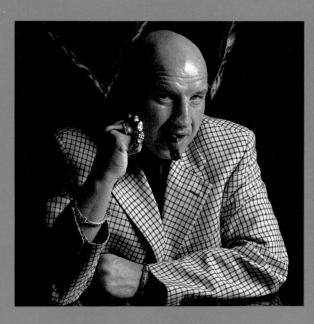

Dave Courtney

Dave Courtney's official job title of "security advisor" seems innocuous enough, but it is as spokesman for London's underworld that he is best known. "Everyone has their preconceptions about me," he explains. "There's been a rumour going round the police here that I'm fortifying my house. Like there's going to be a Waco situation or something!" he chuckles. For a man who clearly revels in this ambiguous role, he appears surprisingly normal. His house is "Base Camp One" for an assortment of friends, family and employees, who come and go all day. Even visiting camera crews and journalists are made welcome by his wife Jennifer, aka club MC Jenny Bean, who happily makes tea and bacon butties for whoever happens to be around. Clearly proud of their home, Courtney says his main inspiration was the court of King Arthur. "The image of the Round Table has always stayed with me." For Courtney, an Englishman's home is most definitely his castle.

Dave Courtneys offizieller Job ist Sicherheitsberater. Das erscheint relativ harmlos. Bekannt wurde er allerdings als Sprecher der Londoner Unterwelt. »Jeder hat seine Meinung über mich«, erhellt er die Sachlage. »Bei der Polizei heißt es, ich würde mein Haus befestigen. Als ob ich darauf warten würde, dass sie es stürmen wie damals in Waco.« Bei dem Gedanken grinst er. Für einen Mann, dem diese ambivalente Rolle eindeutig Vergnügen bereitet, wirkt er gleichzeitig überraschend normal. Sein Haus ist »Base Camp One« – Basiscamp für Freunde, Familienmitglieder und Angestellte, die hier den ganzen Tag ein- und ausgehen. Seine Frau Jennifer, auch bekannt als Club MC Jenny Bean, macht Tee und schmiert für jeden Besucher Schinken-Sandwiches, selbst für Kcamerateams und Journalisten. Auf ihr Haus sind beide sichtlich stolz. Die Tafelrunde von König Artus sei Hauptinspirationsquelle gewesen, sagt Dave Courtney. »Das Bild der Tafelrunde habe ich nie vergessen können.« Für Dave Courtney trifft das klassische Sprichwort im wahrsten Sinne zu: »My home is my castle.«

Below: In the living room, the coat of armour came from a film set and, although a bit of a struggle to put on, it is a perfect fit for Dave. The gruesome head above will eventually become a gargoyle on the roof.
Facing page: Courtney is rarely caught without his signature cigar in hand. The portrait was a surprise gift for his 40th birthday from the many doormen he employs. It was painted by the father of one of them, "Prison trained," Courtney says wryly. Courtney personally oversees all the decoration and is happy to get his hands covered in gold paint and glue to achieve the opulent look he is after.

Ci-dessous: L'armure dans le salon provient d'un plateau de tournage. Bien qu'elle soit un peu difficile à enfiler, elle est parfaitement à la taille de Dave. L'effrayante tête dans l'angle est destinée à devenir une gargouille sur le toit.
Page de droite: difficile de surprendre Courtney sans son célèbre cigare! Son portrait lui a été offert pour ses quarante ans par les nombreux portiers qu'il emploie. Il a été peint par le père de l'un deux, «formé en prison» précise Courtney avec un sourire en coin. Courtney surveille de près tous les travaux de décoration et ne craint pas de se salir les mains avec de la peinture d'or et de la colle afin d'obtenir l'effet opulent qu'il recherche.

Unten: Die Ritterrüstung im Wohnzimmer stammt aus einem Film. Es ist zwar eine Stück harte Arbeit, sich in sie zu zwängen, doch sie paßt Dave perfekt. Der gruselige Kopf darüber wird irgendwann Wasserspeier am Dach des Hauses.
Rechte Seite: Nur selten trifft man Dave Courtney ohne seine typische Zigarre an. Mit diesem Porträt überraschten ihn zu seinem 40. Geburtstag seine zahlreichen Türsteher. Der Vater von einem von ihnen war der Künstler. »Hat er im Gefängnis gelernt«, kommentiert Dave Courtney trocken. Die Dekoration des Hauses überwacht der Hausherr höchstpersönlich. Es macht ihm sogar Spaß, seine Hände mit Goldfarbe und Klebstoff zu beschmutzen, gelingt ihm dabei der opulente Look, nach dem er sucht.

First page: Ceilings are Courtney's thing and he can't understand why most people leave them white: "It's the bit you look at the most, isn't it? So I thought, I'm going to make it the most entertaining bit, give it a bit of opulence." He used multiple decorative borders, gold paint, assorted beads, buttons and trimmings and imported Italian chandeliers to achieve the Monte Carlo look.
Above: A cut-out publicity portrait used for Virgin's in-store promotion of Courtney's book is framed by curtains next to a statue of Humphrey Bogart.

Première page: Les plafonds travaillés sont son dada et il ne comprend pas pourquoi la plupart des gens les laissent blancs: «C'est la partie de la pièce qu'on voit le plus, non? Alors je me suis dit qu'il fallait les rendre plus attrayants, leur donner un peu d'opulence». A l'aide d'une série de corniches ouvragées, de peinture dorée, de perles, de boutons, de galons et de lustres italiens, il leur a donné une allure très «Monte-Carlo».
Ci-dessus: Sur le palier, une silhouette en carton, utilisée comme outil de promotion dans les magasins Virgin pour la sortie du livre de Courtney, tient compagnie à une statue d'Humphrey Bogart.

Eingangsseite: Decken – das sind sein Ding: Dave Courtney versteht nicht, wieso die meisten Menschen sie weiß lassen. »Das ist doch der Teil des Raums, auf den man am meisten blickt, oder? Also wollte ich daraus auch den unterhaltsamsten und interessantesten Bereich machen und ihm etwas Opulenz verleihen.« Für diesen Monte-Carlo-Look verwendet er dekorative Deckenbordüren, Goldfarbe, Perlen, Knöpfe und Behänge sowie aus Italien importierte Lüster.
Oben: Gardinen flankieren einen Aufsteller aus dem Virgin-Store, der für die Promotion von Courtneys Buch verwendet wurde. Daneben eine Statue von Humphrey Bogart.

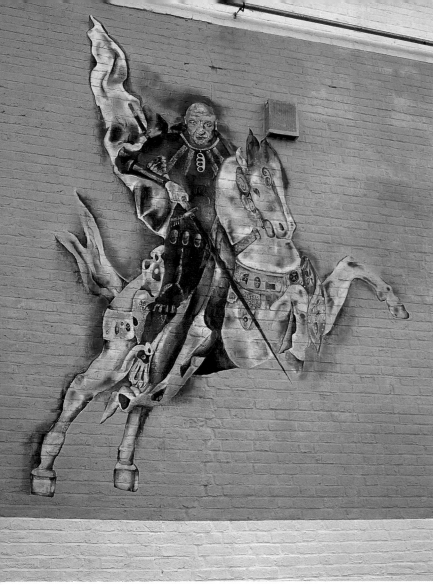

Below: Courtney takes his decorative inspiration from the Court of King Arthur, heraldic imagery and the casinos of Monte-Carlo. The wrought-iron bed, bought in Harrods, takes centre stage in the cream and gold bedroom. Courtney has a wardrobe of clothes to match his theatrical personality, much of it bespoke, like the opulent textured velvet jacket lying on the bed.

Ci-dessus: Courtney s'inspire de la cour du roi Arthur, de l'iconographie héraldique et des casinos de Monte-Carlo. Le lit en fer forgé, acheté chez Harrods, occupe une place centrale dans la chambre beige et or. Courtney possède une garde-robe, généralement faite sur mesure, assortie à sa personnalité haute en couleurs, comme la riche veste en velours jetée sur le lit.

Unten: Seine dekorativen Inspirationen bezieht David Courtney vom Hof von König Artus, aus der mittelalterlichen Heraldik und den Casinos von Monte Carlo. Das gusseiserne Bett stammt von Harrods und nimmt den Mittelpunkt des creme- und goldfarbenen Raums ein. Courtneys zum großen Teil maßgeschneiderte Kleidung entspricht seiner bühnenreifen Erscheinung, wie dieses opulente Samtjacket auf dem Bett.

Facing page: The replica of Doctor Who's "Time machine" police box is "a bit of a piss-take," says Dave. "The naughtiest of the naughty come to this house and it's a nice little surprise for them when they go to use the bathroom!" he chuckles.
Above: When rounding a corner into a quiet residential backstreet in Plumstead, south-east London, the first thing you see is this 30-foot-high mural of Courtney in the role of King Arthur on a charging white horse. It is a taste of what lies beyond.

Page de gauche: La réplique de la cabane de police «Time machine» du Doctor Who est un canular, explique Courtney. «Je reçois chez moi des messieurs très vilains. Ça leur fait toujours un choc quand ils vont au petit coin.»
Ci-dessus: Au détour d'une petite rue tranquille du quartier résidentiel de Plumstead, au sud-est de Londres, on tombe sur cette fresque de neuf mètres de haut, représentant Courtney en roi Arthur chargeant sur son destrier blanc, un avant-goût de ce qui nous attend dans sa maison.

Linke Seite: Die Replik der Police Box »Time machine« aus der britischen Fernsehserie Doctor Who ist eine »Verarschung«, sagt Dave Courtney. »In meinem Haus gehen die bösesten der bösen Buben ein und aus. Und erleben eine kleine Überraschung, wenn sie ins Badezimmer kommen«, grinst er.
Oben: Wenn man in der ruhigen Wohngegend in Plumstead in einem Seitensträßchen um die Ecke biegt, entdeckt man ein neun Meter hohes Wandbild von Courtney als König Artus hoch zu Ross auf einem stürmenden Schimmel – ein erster Vorgeschmack auf das, was einen erwartet.

Ce bijou d'appartement est la demeure de Christian et de Jody de Falbe. Après avoir fréquenté des institutions aussi «british» qu'Eton et Oxford et sans passer par des écoles d'art, Christian s'est fait un nom dans les années 1980 en tant que styliste de la maille, avant de consacrer son talent à la décoration d'intérieur. Son style est aux antipodes du minimalisme et de la retenue, et son amour de la couleur atteint des sommets lyriques. Son salon est peint rouge ketchup de Heinz. Le bleu dragée de sa cuisine à la «Diamants sur canapé» lui a été inspiré par les célèbres emballages du joaillier Tiffany's. Les murs vernis aux tons ambre et miel de sa salle de bains sont censés reproduire «la lumière filtrant au travers d'un flacon de Chanel N°5». On croit rêver! Délibérément kitsch et excentrique, l'appartement est aussi une boîte à idées pour les clients de Christian qui ont des goûts moins exubérants. Christian n'a pas encore trouvé le client de ses rêves, celui qui lui commandera des finitions en peau de léopard peintes à la main ou des murs en graphite... mais l'espoir fait vivre!

Christian de Falbe

This bijou flat with delusions of grandeur is the home of Christian and Jody de Falbe. Sidestepping art school, Christian was educated in the thoroughly British institutions of Eton and Oxford, becoming a knitwear designer of some renown in the 1980s, before he transferred his skills to interior design. His work is an antidote to minimalism and restraint and he loves colour to an almost poetic extreme. In Christian's world, the living room is painted Heinz tomato-sauce red; the sugar-almond blue "Breakfast at Tiffany's" kitchen is inspired by the jeweller's distinctive packaging; and the bathroom is painted in glazed amber and honey tones to resemble "light passing through a Chanel No 5 scent bottle" – how fabulous. Admittedly kitsch and quirky, the flat also provides ideas for clients who have slightly less exuberant tastes. Christian is yet to find his dream client, someone who would want hand-painted leopard-skin finishes and graphite walls – but he lives in hope.

Dieses kleine Juwel ist die Wohnung von Christian und Jody de Falbe. Ohne eine Ausbildung an der Kunsthochschule – vorher hatte Christian de Falbe die durch und durch britischen Institutionen Eton und Oxford durchlaufen – wurde er in den 1980er Jahren als Designer für Strickwaren bekannt. Danach wandte sich Christian de Falbe dem Interior-Design zu, wo er sich nicht gerade durch Mimimalismus oder Zurückhaltung auszeichnet. In Christian de Falbes poetischer Welt schwelgt man in intensiven Farben: Das Wohnzimmer ist in Ketchup-Rot gestrichen, während das Zuckermandelblau der Küche, das sofort an »Frühstück bei Tiffany« denken lässt, von den unverwechselbaren Verpackungen des Juweliers inspiriert ist. Die Bernstein- und Honigtöne im Badezimmer evozieren »den Farbton des Lichts, das durch einen Flakon Chanel No 5 dringt« – einfach hinreißend! Zugegeben: Die Wohnung ist kitschig und exzentrisch, aber sie inspiriert Kunden mit etwas weniger überschäumendem Geschmack. Seinen Traumkunden hat Christian zwar noch nicht gefunden, jemanden, der auf handgemaltem Leopardenfellmuster und grafitgrauen Wänden besteht. Aber er hat die Hoffnung noch nicht aufgegeben.

Previous page: *Christian created the leopard-skin framed mirror. The crowns herald the start of a new collecting passion.*
Above: *With its Osborne & Little striped wallpaper and matching "trompe l'œil" on all four doors and woodwork, this must be the smallest hall in the world to get lost in, but people apparently do.*
Right: *Christian constructed the Brighton Pavilion-inspired mantelpiece in wood and trimmed it with tassels and beads. On the mantel are some of the couple's travel mementos.*

Page précédente: *Christian a créé le cadre de miroir en léopard. Les couronnes inaugurent une nouvelle collection.*
Ci-dessus: *Avec son papier peint à rayures de chez Osborne & Little et ses trompe-l'œil assortis sur les quatre portes et les boiseries, ce doit être le plus petit vestibule du monde où l'on puisse se perdre.*
A droite: *Pour réaliser sa cheminée en bois ornée de glands et de perles, Christian s'est inspiré du Royal Pavilion de Brighton. Sur le manteau de cheminée, des souvenirs de voyage du couple.*

Vorhergehende Seite: *Der Spiegel, dessen Rahmen ein Leopardenfellmuster ziert, ist ein Werk von Christian. Die Kronen signalisieren den Beginn einer neuen Sammelleidenschaft.*
Oben: *Mit gestreiften Tapeten von Osborne & Little und einer dazu passenden Trompe l'œil-Malerei auf allen vier Türen und Holzeinbauten ist dies wohl der kleinste Eingangsbereich der Welt, in dem man sich verlaufen kann.*
Rechts: *Christian entwarf den hölzernen Kaminsims, der an den Royal Pavilion in Brighton erinnert, und dekorierte ihn mit Perlen und Bommeln. Darauf steht eine Auswahl Reiseerinnerungen.*

London Interiors   Christian de Falbe

Quel soulagement de voir, pour une fois, une pop star se comporter en pop star et non en gentleman-farmer, comme c'est si souvent le cas de nos jours! La maison de Noel Gallagher, membre du groupe Oasis, et de sa femme Meg, dans le nord de Londres, a toujours été destinée à devenir l'incarnation de l'esprit rock and roll. Inspirée par de nombreuses nuits passées à visionner des vidéos de James Bond, Super Nova Heights –d'après un de ses songs – est le Graceland de Noel. Les Gallagher ont fait appel à leur ami décorateur Darren Gayer qui les a convaincus de mener leurs idées jusqu'au bout. Un aquarium de trois tonnes et demie, une salle de bains en mosaïque de verre de Venise, un grand lit capitonné en cuir, un tapis violet avec des poils de huit centimètres de long ne sont que quelques-unes de ces idées qu'ils ont concrétisées. C'est lorsqu'il est chez lui que Noel est le plus heureux, une bière à la main, contemplant ses poissons tropicaux ou jouant aux Space Invaders avec des amis dans le studio, qui, bizarrement, n'a encore jamais été utilisé pour enregistrer sa musique.

Noel Gallagher & Meg Matthews

It's such a relief to see a pop star acting like a pop star for a change, instead of a country squire, which so many of them seem to do these days. The north London home of Oasis' Noel Gallagher and his wife Meg Matthews was always going to be the ultimate rock and roll home. Inspired by endless nights of research watching Bond movies on the video, Super Nova Heights is Noel's Graceland. The Gallaghers decided to enlist the help of friend and designer Darren Gayer, who convinced them to push their ideas to the limit. A three-and-a-half-ton fish tank, Venetian glass mosaic bathroom, leather sleigh bed and three-inch-deep purple shag pile are just some of the ideas that became a reality. When at home, Noel is at his happiest, beer in hand, watching his tropical fish, or playing Space Invaders with friends in the studio, which curiously he has never actually used for recording.

Es ist sehr erfrischend, einen Popstar zu sehen, der sich auch wie ein Popstar benimmt – und nicht wie ein Landedelmann, wie das heute so viele von ihnen tun. Das in Nord-London gelegene Zuhause von Noel Gallagher (Oasis) und seiner Frau Meg sollte schon immer das ultimative Rock'n'Roll-Heim werden. Zahllose Nächte wurden mit der Suche nach dem richtigen Stil verbracht – dank Bond-Filmen auf Video ist Super Nova Heights – nach einem seiner Songs benannt – Noel Gallaghers Graceland. Das Ehepaar entschied sich, ihren Freund, den Designer Darren Gayer, mit ins kreative Boot zu nehmen, der sie wiederum überzeugte, ihre Wünsche auch kompromisslos auszuleben. Ein 3,5 Tonnen schweres Aquarium, ein Badezimmer aus venezianischem Glasmosaik, ein Lederbett und ein acht Zentimeter tiefer Kuschelteppich in tiefstem Lila sind nur einige der Ideen, die verwirklicht wurden. Zu Hause ist Noel Gallagher am glücklichsten, wenn er – ein Bier in der Hand – seine tropischen Fische beobachten oder im Studio mit Freunden Space Invaders spielen kann. Für Musikaufnahmen hat er das Studio kurioserweise noch nie benutzt.

Previous pages, left: *Meg Matthews having a laugh with friend and interior designer Darren Gayer.*
Previous pages, right: *Noel's studio at the top of the house had previously been three bedrooms with low ceilings. The Gallaghers' vast collection of pop memorabilia includes a Mellotron.*
Above: *The 14-foot-long, three-and-a-half-ton fish tank divides the living room and the hallway.*
Right: *some of Noel's many music awards.*
Facing page: *the hall.*

Double page précédente, à gauche: *Meg Matthews plaisantant avec son décorateur et ami Darren Gayer.*
Double page précédente, à droite: *Le studio de Noel au dernier étage, qui accueillait autrefois trois chambres au plafond bas. La vaste collection d'objets rock and roll de Gallagher comprend un Mellotron.*
Ci-dessus: *L'aquarium de plus de quatre mètres de long sépare le salon de l'entrée.*
A droite: *une partie des nombreux trophées musicaux de Noel.*
Page de droite: *l'entrée.*

Vorhergehende Doppelseite, links: *Meg Matthews und ihr guter Freund, der Innenarchitekt Darren Gayer, sind guter Stimmung.*
Vorhergehende Doppelseite, rechts: *Früher befanden sich in Noel Gallaghers Studio unter dem Dach des Hauses drei Schlafzimmer mit niedrigen Decken. Die umfangreiche Sammlung, die die Gallaghers zum Thema Pop-Memorabilien zusammengetragen haben, beinhaltet auch ein Mellotron.*
Oben: *3,5 Tonnen schwer und mehr als vier Meter lang ist das Aquarium, das Wohnzimmer und Flur voneinander trennt.*
Rechts: *eine kleine Auswahl an Preisen, mit denen Noel Gallagher ausgezeichnet wurde.*
Rechte Seite: *der Eingangsbereich.*

Facing page: *The 1960s pink leather chairs on the mezzanine level of the studio were designed for a member of the Swedish royal family. Noel has never recorded at Super Nova Heights, preferring instead to hang out in the studio with his mates and to play on an original pub Space Invaders game, a present from Meg for his 30th birthday.*
Above: *An over-the-top button-backed leather sleigh bed was originally going to be purple. The Diptyque candles were a gift from their friend Naomi Campbell.*
Right: *Noel's passion for the 1960s inspired the target bath, which was moulded in fibreglass and clad in Venetian mosaic tiles.*

Page de gauche: *Les fauteuils des années 1960 en cuir rose sur la mezzanine du studio ont été créés pour un membre de la famille royale de Suède. Noel n'a jamais enregistré dans son studio, il s'en sert pour s'amuser avec ses amis.*
Ci-dessus: *A l'origine, l'extravagant lit en cuir noir capitonné devait être violet. Les bougies de la maison Diptyque leur ont été offertes par leur amie Naomi Campbell.*
A droite: *la baignoire était moulée d'abord en fibres de verre et ornée de mosaïque en verre de Venise.*

Linke Seite: *Die in pinkfarbenem Leder bezogenen Sessel stammen aus den 1960er Jahren und wurden damals für ein Mitglied des schwedischen Königshauses angefertigt. Sie stehen im Mezzanin des Studios, das Noel Gallagher noch nie als solches genutzt hat – hierhin zieht er sich mit seinen Kumpels zurück und spielt das Spiel Space Invaders.*
Oben: *Das in der Form an einen Schlitten erinnernde und wie ein Chesterfield-Sofa mit Knöpfen überzogene Bett sollte ursprünglich lila sein. Die Kerzen der Firma Diptyque sind ein Geschenk ihrer Freundin Naomi Campbell.*
Rechts: *Das Bad wurde erst in Fiberglas gegossen und dann mit venezianischen Mosaikstückchen bedeckt.*

David Gill a découvert cet immense espace industriel il y a quelques années. «Le bâtiment était si beau», explique-t-il, «que j'ai été envahi par une émotion qui me collait au corps». Aussi, Gill, jusque-là accro impénitent aux quartiers branchés de l'ouest de Londres, a traversé la Tamise vers le sud pour s'installer à Vauxhall. Aujourd'hui, c'est devenu le plus beau showroom de meubles de la capitale, l'équivalent en arts décoratifs de la galerie Saatchi. Gill vit «au-dessus de la boutique», dans une série de pièces à géométrie variable séparées des principaux espaces d'exposition et des bureaux. Si l'immeuble est attrayant, on ne peut en dire autant du quartier. On n'y trouve que d'anciennes fabriques et ateliers, de vastes systèmes de circulation et des HLM. Mais, comme dit Gill: «Il faut bien que quelqu'un se lance». De fait, l'endroit est si bien relié au West End qu'il ne tardera sans doute pas à prendre son envol. Gill ayant une capacité hors du commun à détecter les nouveaux talents du design, il y a fort à parier qu'il ne se trompe pas non plus au sujet de Vauxhall.

David Gill

When David Gill came across this enormous light-industrial space a few years ago, he was overcome by its potential. "The building was so beautiful," he says, "it had a feeling I just couldn't forget." So Gill, the consummate urbane West Londoner, decamped south of the river to Vauxhall. Today it is undoubtedly the best furniture showroom in the capital, the decorative arts equivalent of the Saatchi Gallery. Gill lives "above the shop" in a series of versatile rooms that are separate from the main gallery spaces and office. While the building's attractions are obvious, the area's are not. It's a pocket of the city that the developers seem to have overlooked, being a tract of light-industrial buildings, vast traffic systems and council housing. But Gill rationalises: "Someone has to pioneer an area," arguing that its accessibility to the West End is so obviously appealing that it's only a matter of time before the area takes off.

Als er vor einigen Jahren dieses riesige Fabrikgebäude entdeckte, war David Gill von dem sich eröffnenden Potential schier überwältigt. »Das Gebäude besaß Schönheit und vermittelte ein Gefühl, das ich einfach nicht vergessen konnte«, sagt er. Und so kam es, dass David Gill, der typische Stadtbewohner von West-London, südlich des Flusses in Vauxhall sein neues Lager aufschlug. Heute hat sich das Lager zum besten Möbel-Showroom der Stadt gemausert – quasi das dekorative Kunst-Pendant zur Kunstgalerie von Charles Saatchi. Nach alter Tradition wohnt der Inhaber über seinem Laden, in einer vielseitig verwendbaren Zimmerflucht, die separat vom Ausstellungsraum und dem Büro liegt. Mögen die Vorzüge des Gebäudes offensichtlich sein, die der Gegend sind es nicht. Die Stadtentwickler jedenfalls scheinen diesen kleinen Stadtteil übersehen zu haben – diesen Streifen von Leichtindustriebauten, ausgedehnten Verkehrsadern und sozialem Wohnungsbau. Aber, so betrachtet David Gill mit Vernunft die Lage: »Irgendjemand muss ja den Anfang machen.« Die Nähe zum West End sei jedenfalls ein riesiger Vorteil, sodass es nur noch eine Frage der Zeit sei, bevor Vauxhall zum neuen Trend wird.

Previous page: The vast scale of Gill's main exhibition space lends a surreal quality to Garouste & Bonetti's furniture. The double-sided yellow gold-leaf mirror, hanging from an enormous chain, is reminiscent of an oversized piece of jewellery.
Right: a cabinet by Jean Prouvé in aluminium, coated steel and oak.
Below: In the foreground, the 1920s chair came from couturier Norman Hartnell's showroom. The wedged shoes are by Abigail Lane and have Gill's foot imprint inside. In front of a photograph of Kate Moss by Wolfgang Tillmans is a chair originally from the apartment which Le Corbusier built in Paris for Charles de Beistegui.

Page précédente: L'échelle démesurée de la principale salle d'exposition de Gill confère une qualité irréelle aux meubles de Garouste & Bonetti; le miroir à deux faces dans un cadre doré à la feuille et suspendu au bout d'une chaîne évoque un bijou géant.
A droite: un cabinet de Jean Prouvé en aluminium, feuilles d'acier et chêne.
Ci-dessous: Au premier plan, le fauteuil des années 1920 vient du showroom du couturier Norman Hartnell. Les chaussures à semelles compensées sont d'Abigail Lane. Devant une photographie de Kate Moss par Wolfgang Tillmans, un fauteuil provenant de l'appartement parisien que Le Corbusier a construit pour Charles de Beistegui.

Vorhergehende Seite: Die riesigen Dimensionen von David Gills Hauptausstellungsraum verleihen dem Mobiliar von Garouste & Bonetti etwas Surreales. Der doppelseitige Spiegel mit Blattgoldrahmen hängt an einer überlangen Kette und erinnert an ein überdimensionales Schmuckstück.
Rechts: eine Kommode von Jean Prouvé, gefertigt aus Aluminium, Eiche und Stahlblech.
Unten: Im Vordergrund steht ein Stuhl aus den 1920er Jahren. Er stammt aus dem Showroom des Modeschöpfers Norman Hartnell. Die Plateauschuhe sind von Abigail Lane. Vor einer Tillmans-Fotografie von Kate Moss steht ein Sessel aus dem Pariser Apartment, das Le Corbusier für den Sammler Charles de Beistegui gebaut hatte.

Above: At the entrance to the L-shaped living space is a cabinet called "Love-slave box" by artist Richard Sneyder. The vase is by multi-disciplined artist Stephanie Bergman. Sarah Lucas' "Bunny gets snookered" chair sits below a celestial painting, "Passion of Origins", by John Murphy.
Right: a view through the 1960s fibreglass and leather chair to a deep blue powder-coated aluminium stool by Donald Judd that Gill uses as a coffee table. It stands in front of a 1935 sofa by Eugène Printz, which is covered in hand-embroidered gold and green silk thread on aubergine silk velvet.

Ci-dessus: A l'entrée de la salle de séjour en L, un cabinet de l'artiste Richard Sneyder, baptisé «Boîte d'esclave de l'amour». Le vase est signé de l'artiste pluridisciplinaire Stephanie Bergman. Une chaise de Sarah Lucas, «Bunny se fait aplatir» est placée sous un tableau céleste de John Murphy «Passion des origines».
A droite: Vu à travers un fauteuil en fibres de verre et cuir des années 1960, un tabouret en aluminium enduit de poudre bleu nuit, œuvre de Donald Judd, que Gill utilise en guise de table basse. Il se tient devant ur sofa d'Eugène Printz, de 1935.

Oben: Am Eingang zum L-förmig geschnittenen Wohnzimmer steht eine als »Love-slave box« titulierte Kommode des Künstlers Richard Sneyder. Die Vase darauf stammt von Stephanie Bergman, einer in vielen Disziplinen arbeitenden Künstlerin. Sarah Lucas' »Bunny gets snookered«-Stuhl steht unter einem Gemälde »Passion of Origins« von John Murphy.
Rechts: Blick durch einen Sessel aus Fiberglas und Leder aus den 1960er Jahren auf einen pulverbeschichteten tiefblauen Aluminiumstuhl von Donald Judd, den David Gill jedoch als Couchtisch verwendet. Das Sofa wurde 1935 von Eugène Printz entworfen.

Clockwise from top left: *a corner of the main living space; view of the stairs; Gill has used a light-filled "conservatory room" to display furniture by Oriel Harwood constructed in moulded stone composite and "scagliola" – which is a mixture of glue, powdered marble and pigment; in the entrance hall, a sculptural, almost cinematic screen has colour emanating from behind.*

Du haut à gauche, dans le sens des aiguilles d'une montre: *un coin de la salle de séjour; vue de l'escalier; dans cette pièce inondée de lumière, baptisée «la serre», Gill expose les meubles composites d'Oriel Harwood en pierre moisie et «scagliola», un mélange de colle, de poudre de marbre et de pigments; dans le vestibule, l'écran sculptural, presque cinématographique, est éclairé par derrière.*

Im Uhrzeigersinn von links oben: *eine Ecke des großen Wohnzimmers; Blick auf die Treppe; in einem lichtdurchfluteten »Wintergarten« sind Möbel von Oriel Harwood ausgestellt. Sie wurden aus Gussverbundstein und »Scagliola« – zerstoßener Marmor, Kleister und Pigment – gefertigt; die Wand im Eingangsbereich, die einer Art Kinoleinwand gleicht, wird von hinten beleuchtet.*

London Interiors   David Gill

Clockwise from top left: A lamp by Garouste & Bonetti sits on a prototype table by Jasper Morrison; the rendered bench along the walls of the enormous chamber-like bathroom allows Gill to shower sitting down; in the dining area, one of Marc Francis' "compression paintings"; a model of a rooftop duplex building, which will be Gill's next building project.

Du haut à gauche, dans le sens des aiguilles d'une montre: une lampe de Garouste & Bonetti sur un prototype de table de Jasper Morrison; dans l'immense salle de bains, le banc enduit qui court le long des murs permet à Gill de se doucher assis; dans le coin salle à manger, une «peinture compression» de Marc Francis; la maquette du prochain projet de Gill: un immeuble avec un duplex sur le toit.

Im Uhrzeigersinn von links oben: Auf einem Tischprototyp von Jasper Morrison steht eine Lampe von Garouste & Bonetti; auf dem glatt verputzten Vorsprung kann man sich im Sitzen duschen; im Essbereich hängt ein »Compression Painting« von Marc Francis; das Modell einer zweistöckigen Dachterrassenwohnung – Gills neuestes Bauvorhaben.

Vauxhall, London SE1

On ne s'attend pas à trouver l'artiste David Harrison dans un HLM du East End. Au bout d'un escalier en béton sale et sombre, son appartement est une oasis dorée dans un désert gris et brutal. Derrière une palissade en bois blanc et un portail à verrou s'ouvre un autre monde rempli d'une cacophonie de couleurs, de fleurs lumineuses, de poupées en plastique et de caniches teints en tons pastels. Harrison refaçonne sans cesse son univers fantastique, à l'aide de bric et de broc trouvés dans des brocantes ou sur le trottoir, dorant souvent le tout à la bombe. La station balnéaire de Blackpool, sur les rives de la mer d'Irlande, est sa Mecque spirituelle et créative avec son abondance de trésors architecturaux tarabiscotés et ses souvenirs kitsch pour touristes. Harrison rêve que sa dépouille mortelle soit exposée un jour dans la salle de bal de la fameuse tour. «Un orchestre jouera du Prokofiev, du Khatchatourian et du Tchaïkovsky et des dames en crinolines danseront la valse autour de mon cercueil rose tapissé de léopard dans lequel je serai couché dans ma grenouillère de bordel».

David Harrison

An East End housing estate is the unlikely location of the home of artist David Harrison. Reached by a grimy and gloomy concrete stairwell, the flat is a golden oasis in a brutal, grey land. Through white picket fences and a latched gate another world unfolds, filled with clashing colour, luminous flowers, plastic dolls and pastel-coloured poodles. Harrison creates and recreates his fantastical surroundings, using any old scraps picked up in junk shops or off the street, often spraying the whole lot gold. The northern seaside town of Blackpool is his spiritual and creative Mecca, with its abundance of ornate architectural treasures and tacky tourist trash. Harrison dreams of being allowed to lie in state in the Tower ballroom when he dies. "An orchestra will be playing Prokofiev, Khachaturian and Tchaikovsky, and ladies with enormous dresses will be waltzing around the pink, leopard skin-lined coffin, in which I will be lying in my brothel creepers."

Eine Wohnung wie die des Künstlers David Harrison würde man in dem Häuserblock im Londoner East End, der aus der Zeit des sozialen Wohnungsbaus stammt, nicht erwarten. Über ein verlottertes, trübsinniges Treppenhaus aus Beton gelangt man in die Wohnung, eine goldene Oase mitten in einer brutalen, grauen Wüste. Hinter einem weißen Palisadenzaun und einem verriegelten Tor erschließt sich eine andere Welt, voller schriller Farben, leuchtender Blumen, Plastikpuppen und pastellfarbener Pudel. Diese fantastisch-fantasievolle Umgebung schafft sich Harrison mit noch dem kleinsten Fundstück vom Trödel oder Sperrmüll, die er oft ganz und gar mit Goldlack besprüht. Das Seebad Blackpool im Norden des Landes ist sein spirituelles und kreatives Mekka. Dort herrscht wahrer Überfluss an überladenen architektonischen Schätzen und billigem Touristenramsch. Harrison träumt davon, nach seinem Tod im Ballsaal des Tower aufgebahrt zu werden. »Ein Orchester spielt Prokofjew, Khachaturian und Tschaikowsky. Ladies in raumfüllender Abendrobe tanzen Walzer um den pinkfarbenen, mit Leopardenfell ausgekleideten Sarg, in dem ich mit meinen Leisetretern liege.«

Previous page: the golden dining room, filled with a mélange of animal prints and plastic dolls.
Right and below: The living room, like the rest of the flat, is furnished with finds from skips and junk shops, some of which are also used in David's sculptures. "Bittern eating Bird", constructed from rusty garden shears, a plastic doll and a nest of twigs, stands in front of the fire. "David's Award" – the lips of Michelangelo's statue mounted on a sewage pipe, all sprayed gold – is Harrison's ironic take on the absurdity of the artworld establishment.

Page précédente: la salle à manger dorée, décorée avec un mélange détonnant d'imprimés animaliers et de poupées en plastique.
A droite et ci-dessous: Le salon, comme le reste de l'appartement, est meublé de trouvailles dénichées dans des bennes à ordures ou des brocantes. On en retrouve certaines dans les sculptures de David. Devant la cheminée, «Butor dévorant un oiseau», construit avec un sécateur rouillé, une poupée en plastique et un nid de brindilles. Le «Trophée de David», les lèvres de la statue de Michel-Ange montées sur un tuyau d'égout, le tout doré à la bombe, est un commentaire ironique sur l'absurdité de l'establishment artistique.

Vorhergehende Seite: das goldene Esszimmer, angefüllt mit einer Melange aus Tierfellmustern und Plastikpuppen.
Rechts und oben: Wie die restliche Wohnung ist auch das Wohnzimmer mit Fundstücken aus Trödelläden angefüllt. Einige der Stücke werden auch in Davids Skulpturen verwendet: »Bittern eating Bird« aus rostigen Gartenscheren, einer Plastikpuppe und einem Nest aus Zweigen steht vor dem Kamin. Mit »David's Award«, einem goldbesprühten Konstrukt aus den Lippen von Michelangelos David auf einem Abflussrohr, karikiert Harrison die Absurdität des Establishments in der Kunstwelt.

London Interiors   David Harrison

The peeling wallpaper in the bedroom was first painted over in rich fuchsia and then sprayed with gold spots. A functional cupboard has been given the Harrison treatment with more gold paint and the application of gilded dolls and plastic fruit. The poodle painting and the gilt-framed "Rococo Eye" are also by Harrison. Only the prosaic modern window frames give away the housing-estate location.

Le papier peint en lambeaux dans la chambre à coucher a d'abord été repeint en fuchsia avant d'être parsemé de taches d'or. Une armoire tout bête a été revue et corrigée à la Harrison avec de la peinture, des poupées et des fruits en plastique dorés. Le portrait de caniche et «l'œil rococo» dans des cadres dorés sont également signés Harrison. Seuls les montants de fenêtres prosaïques révèlent que l'appartement se trouve dans un HLM.

Die sich lösende Schlafzimmertapete wurde in einem tiefen Fuchsienrot überstrichen und dann mit aufgesprühten Goldtupfen verziert. Einem funktionellen Schrank wurde ebenfalls das »Harrison treatment« verpaßt: Goldfarbe und applizierte vergoldete Püppchen und Plastikfrüchte. Das Pudelbild und »Rococo Eye« im vergoldeten Rahmen stammen auch von Harrison. Nur die einfallslosen modernen Fensterrahmen erinnern den Betrachter an das Umfeld des sozialen Wohnungsbaus.

Below: Behind a beaded curtain, the tiny kitchen is crammed full with junk-shop furniture and a pink-painted 1930s fridge. "Garpoodles", rather than gargoyles, look down from the top of the silver-painted, Chrysler-building-inspired wardrobe.
Facing page: Harrison finds as much to delight him in a cheap plastic Barbie as he does in a priceless medieval wall painting. His bathroom is piled high with an assortment of dolls against a fishy wallpaper background.

Ci-dessous: Derrière un rideau de perles, la minuscule cuisine est bondée de meubles de brocante et d'un réfrigérateur des années 1930 repeint en rose. Des «Caniches gargouilles» trônent au sommet d'une penderie peinte en argent et inspirée du Chrysler Building de Manhattan.
Page de droite: Harrison est aussi émerveillé par une Barbie en plastique à deux sous que par une fresque médiévale sans prix. Dans sa salle de bains, un assortiment de poupées s'empile sur un fond de papier peint aquatique.

Unten: Hinter einem Vorhang aus Perlen verbirgt sich die winzige Küche, die vollgestopft ist mit Möbeln vom Trödler und einem pinkfarben gestrichenen Kühlschrank aus den 1930er Jahren. Moderne Wasserspeier in Form von Pudeln gucken vom »Dach« des silbergetönten Schranks, dessen Form vom New Yorker Chrysler Building inspiriert wurde.
Rechte Seite: Einer billigen Barbiepuppe aus Plastik kann David Harrison genauso viel abgewinnen wie einem unbezahlbaren Wandgemälde aus dem Mittelalter. In seinem Bad stapelt sich eine Puppensammlung vor einer Tapete mit Fischmotiven.

Above: In the dining room, Harrison stands by the shrine he built to his beloved poodle, Hoover, with whom he had shared the flat for ten years. Hoover, whose ashes are now safely installed in a china poodle on the shrine, was dyed fluorescent pink and at one time briefly sported a purple coat with yellow and orange spots.

Ci-dessus: Dans la salle à manger, Harrison pose près de l'autel érigé à son cher caniche Hoover, avec lequel il a partagé son appartement pendant dix ans. Hoover, dont les cendres reposent à présent dans un caniche en porcelaine, était teint en rose fluo et a porté pendant une brève saison un manteau violet à petits pois jaunes et orange.

Oben: David Harrison im Wohnzimmer vor dem Schrein, den er seinem geliebten Pudel Hoover errichtet hat. Mit ihm teilte er sich die Wohnung zehn Jahre lang. Jetzt ist seine Asche sicher in einem Porzellanpudel untergebracht, der auf dem Altar steht. Zu Lebzeiten trug Hoover sein Fell in fluoreszierendem Pink, für kurze Zeit allerdings auch in Lila mit gelben und orangefarbenen Tupfen.

En matière de projet de maison individuelle, la relation fragile entre le client et l'architecte est notoirement houleuse. Toutefois, Nick Hastings et Denise Hurst n'ont pas à s'en plaindre. Les deux ans qui se sont écoulés entre l'achat de leur maison à l'ouest londonien et le moment où ils ont pu «y vivre convenablement» n'ont en rien entamé leur admiration pour Louisa Hutton, qui représente une moitié du cabinet d'architectes Sauerbruch & Hutton. Les travaux de la demeure classée ont été réalisés en tenant surtout compte des enfants: tout ce dont ils ont besoin, des céréales pour leur petit déjeuner à l'ordinateur, leur est accessible sans l'aide d'un adulte. Les Hastings ont également souhaité un environnement neutre, d'abord pour pouvoir exposer leurs œuvres d'art, puis afin qu'il évolue avec eux. Denise affirme sans hésitation que Louisa «a créé la plus magnifique des maisons de famille».

Nick Hastings & Denise Hurst

On domestic projects, the fragile relationship between client and architect is notoriously challenging. But the owners of this West London house, Nick Hastings and Denise Hurst, have a happy ending to report. Even the two years it took from purchase to "properly living there" hasn't diminished their admiration for Louisa Hutton, one half of Sauerbruch & Hutton. The listed interior of the house was designed very much with their children in mind; everything they need, from breakfast cereals to the computer, is accessible without adults having to be present. The Hastings also wanted a neutral background, firstly to display their art, but also to allow the place to evolve as they live in it. Denise states without hesitation that "Louisa has created the most wonderful family home ever."

Die zarten Bande zwischen Innenarchitekt und Kunden sind bekanntermaßen gerade dann sehr angespannt, wenn es um das eigene Heim geht. Doch Nick Hastings und Denise Hurst, Besitzer dieses Hauses im Westen Londons, haben ein Happy End erlebt. Selbst die zwei Jahre Wartezeit zwischen Hauskauf und dem endgültigen Einzug haben ihrer Bewunderung für Louisa Hutton vom Team Sauerbruch & Hutton keinen Abbruch getan. Das unter Denkmalschutz stehende Haus wurde vor allem mit Blick auf die Kinder renoviert – alles, was sie brauchen, ob nun Frühstücksmüsli oder Computer, ist auch ohne Anwesenheit der Eltern zugänglich. Ferner wollten die Hastings einen neutralen Hintergrund: erstens, um ihre Kunst auszustellen, zweitens, um ihrem Heim die Möglichkeit zur eigenen Entwicklung zu geben. Ohne Zögern sagt Denise Hurst, dass »Louisa Hutton das schönste Familienheim entworfen hat, das es überhaupt gibt!«

Previous page: *Florence, the youngest of the Hastings' three daughters, dressed in Cookie clothing, which Denise designs.*
Above: *The vast concrete-slab table in the dining room is the heart of the house. Above the Charlotte Perriand and Jean Prouvé sideboard is a cibachrome photograph of découpage by Sarah Charlesworth. The white leather shoes were Denise's in the 1960s.*
Right: *two oil and textile diptychs by Yinka Shonibare.*
Facing page: *the kitchen island.*

Page précédente: *Florence, la benjamine des trois filles des Hastings, porte des vêtements Cookie, créations de Denise.*
Ci-dessus: *Dans la salle à manger, la grande table couverte d'un plateau en béton est le cœur de la maison. Au-dessus de la desserte de Charlotte Perriand et Jean Prouvé, une photographie en cibachrome d'un découpage de Sarah Charlesworth.*
A droite: *deux diptyques à l'huile et en tissu de Yinka Shonibare.*
Page de droite: *l'îlot central de la cuisine.*

Vorhergehende Seite: *Florence, die jüngste der drei Töchter, ist in Cookie gekleidet – der Modefirma ihrer Mutter Denise Hurst.*
Oben: *Der riesige Esstisch aus Beton ist zum Herzstück des Hauses geworden. Über der Kommode von Charlotte Perriand und Jean Prouvé hängt eine Decoupage eines Cibachromefotos von Sarah Charlesworth.*
Rechts: *zwei Ölfarbe- und Textil-Diptychen von Yinka Shonibare.*
Rechte Seite: *die Kücheninsel.*

Clockwise from top left: *the practical storage system in the glass atrium at the back of the house; the living room is dominated by a huge sheepskin rug; Nick's shower room has a glass roof and pebble-covered floor; Sauerbruch and Hutton designed a vast storage unit to house the television, hi-fi and fridge in the living room.*

Du haut à gauche, dans le sens des aiguilles d'une montre: *L'atrium en verre à l'arrière de la maison est doté d'un système de rangement; dans le salon, un immense tapis en poils de mouton; la douche de Nick a un toit en verre et un sol en galets; Sauerbruch et*

Hutton ont dessiné l'immense placard du salon qui abrite la télévision, le réfrigérateur et la hi-fi.

Im Uhrzeigersinn von links oben: *ein praktisches Aufbewahrungssystem im Glasatrium an der Rückseite des Hauses; das Wohnzimmer wird von einem riesigen Teppich aus Schaffell dominiert; Nicks Dusche verfügt über ein Glasdach und einen mit Kieselsteinen ausgelegten Boden; für Fernsehen, Musikanlage und Kühlschrank entwarfen Sauerbruch und Hutton im Wohnzimmer ein geräumiges Aufbewahrungssystem.*

London Interiors Nick Hastings & Denise Hurst

The children's playroom is on the lower level of the glass atrium. Dalsouple rubber flooring runs from the interior through to the garden. The laundry room is linked to the playroom by a window slot, which allows whoever is doing the laundry to keep an eye on the children. All the pictures are in frames designed and decorated by Denise using coloured paints and sequins.

La salle de jeux se trouve sous la verrière. Le tapis en caoutchouc s'étend jusque dans le jardin. La buanderie est reliée à la salle de jeux par une fenêtre étroite qui permet de garder un œil sur les enfants tout en faisant la lessive. Tous les cadres des dessins d'enfants ont été réalisés par Denise et décorés de peintures et de paillettes.

Das Spielzimmer der Kinder liegt im unteren Geschoss des Glasatriums. Im ganzen Haus bis zum Garten sind Kautschukböden verlegt. Das Bügelzimmer ist mit dem Spielzimmer durch einen Fensterschlitz verbunden. Wer immer sich um die Wäsche kümmert, kann also gleichzeitig die Geschehnisse im Kinderzimmer unter Kontrolle behalten. Die Rahmen aller Bilder hat Denise Hurst selbst entworfen und mit unterschiedlichen Farben und Pailletten dekoriert.

Sera Hersham-Loftus, décoratrice et créatrice des lampes «Rude», a deux passions, l'opéra et le ballet – elle dansait autrefois dans la compagnie Israeli. Elle a aménagé sa maison à colonnades dans le quartier de St. John's Wood dans un style qui, à première vue, s'accorde mal avec une petite famille. En entrant, on a du mal à imaginer une marmaille chahutant dans un tel décor. Néanmoins, la politique de la maison est aux antipodes du «Regarde mais ne touche à rien». Même la précieuse table Louis Quatorze est traitée sans révérence particulière. On trouve souvent les enfants confortablement installés sur des piles de soieries et de velours édouardiens dans le petit salon, faisant consciencieusement leurs devoirs. Cœur de la maison, la cuisine est dominée par une immense table de réfectoire 19°, entourée de bancs et de chaises rachetés à une synagogue. Au plafond, un lustre que Sera a dessiné en intégrant les branches du vieux saule pleureur du jardin, mort et abattu.

Sera Hersham-Loftus

Sera Hersham-Loftus, decorator and creator of "Rude" lamps, was once a dancer with the Israeli Ballet and ballet as well as opera remain two of her greatest passions. In this pillar-fronted house, in St. John's Wood, she has created an unlikely home for a young family. When entering, it's hard to imagine children in such an environment, but this is emphatically not a "look but don't touch" set-up; even the most delicate Louis Quatorze table is treated irreverently. The children can often be found ensconced in a pile of Edwardian velvets and silks on the dressing-room floor, wrapped up in the down-to-earth pursuit of homework. The kitchen is the nucleus of the home, dominated by a huge 19th-century refectory table, surrounded by benches and chairs bought from a West End synagogue. A chandelier designed by Sera is enmeshed in a contorted willow that was cut down from the garden.

Früher gehörte die Interior-Designerin Sera Hersham-Loftus, die mit ihren »Rude«-Lampen bekannt geworden ist, dem Ensemble des israelischen Staatsballetts an. Immer noch sind Oper und Ballett ihre großen Leidenschaften. In einem mit Pilastern geschmückten Haus im viktorianischen Stadtteil St. John's Wood hat sie ein ungewöhnliches Heim für eine junge Familie geschaffen. Zunächst kann man sich hier Kinder nur schwer vorstellen, doch in der häuslichen Atmosphäre gilt keineswegs »Berühren verboten!«, und selbst der empfindlichste Louis-Quatorze-Tisch wird respektlos behandelt. Oft lassen sich die Kinder zwischen edwardianischen Samt- und Seidenstoffen auf dem Boden des Ankleidezimmers häuslich nieder und machen, ganz bodenständig, Schularbeiten. Die Küche ist das Herz des Hauses und wird von einem riesigen Refektoriumstisch aus dem 19. Jahrhundert sowie Bänken und Stühlen beherrscht, die aus einer Synagoge aus dem West End stammen. Über allem hängt ein Kronleuchter, von Sera entworfen, zwischen den knorrigen Ästen einer Weide, die im Garten gefällt wurde.

First page: Sara reclines on her four-poster bed draped with antique
damasks, silks and lace.
Above: Beaded peplums disguise the light switches which control the
Fortuny wall lamps, while Venice was the inspiration for the water-
coloured walls.
Right: Sara's passion for antique fashion and textiles is evident in
every corner of the house. In the living room an embroidered silk
shawl decorates a child's iron bed.

Première page: Sera, assise sur son lit à baldaquin drapé de dentelles,
de soieries et de damas anciens.
Ci-dessus: Des cascades de perles cachent les interrupteurs qui contrô-
lent les appliques Fortuny. Les murs aux tons d'aquarelles sont d'inspiration vénitienne.
A droite: Le moindre recoin de la maison témoigne de la passion de
Sera pour les meubles et les tissus anciens. Dans le grand salon, un
châle en soie brodée orne un lit d'enfant en fer.

Eingangsseite: Sera entspannt sich auf dem Himmelbett, das mit alten Damast- und Seidenstoffen sowie Spitze dekoriert ist.
Oben: Hinter den Perlengehängen verstecken sich die Lichtschalter
für die Fortuny-Wandlampen. Venezianische Vorbilder lieferten die Inspiration für die aquarellierten Wände.
Rechts: Die Leidenschaft Sera Hersham-Loftus' für Retromode und
antike Stoffe spürt man in jedem Winkel des Hauses. Der bestickte
Seidenschal liegt als dekoratives Element auf einem eisernen Kinder-
bett im Wohnzimmer.

London Interiors   Sera Hersham-Loftus

Lorsqu'on entre dans l'extraordinaire appartement de Peter Hone dans l'ouest de Londres, on est accueilli par Mr. Brown, un jack- russell débordant d'énergie, et par le riche parfum d'automne du chutney qui mijote sur le feu dans la cuisine. Hone a une formation de cuisinier mais, aujourd'hui, il puise son plus grand plaisir dans ce qu'il appelle sa «collection de chaos organisé». Celle-ci recouvre pratiquement toutes les surfaces visibles, le plafond lui-même ne tardera pas à être englouti sous les précieux plâtres ouvragés. Les couleurs neutres de la pierre créent une atmosphère quasi onirique. On se croirait flottant au-dessus d'un jardin de corail. Chaque pièce est unique mais la collection s'apprécie dans son ensemble. C'est sans doute du lit à baldaquin que l'on a la meilleure vue sur l'étendue du trésor de M. Hone. Lorsqu'on émet l'hypothèse d'un déménagement de sa collection, celui-ci s'exclame: «Jamais! Je me ferai mouler dans du plâtre, portant mes pantalons en velours côtelé préférés, et je resterai ici au centre de cette pièce, pour l'éternité!»

Peter Hone

On entering Peter Hone's extraordinary West London flat, one is greeted first by Mr Brown, an enthusiastic Jack Russell, and then by a rich autumnal smell, emanating from the kitchen, of homemade chutney. Hone originally trained as a chef, but today his greatest delight comes from what he calls his "collection of organised chaos", which covers every available surface. Even the ceiling is soon to be engulfed by priceless, ornately worked plaster. The neutral stone colours create a dreamlike environment, in which one almost seems to float over a coral garden, where each piece is unique, but the landscape is seen as a whole. The four-poster bed would be the perfect vantage point from which to view Mr Hone's wealth of treasures. Wondering how it would ever be possible to move the collection elsewhere, Peter exclaims: "Oh never! I will be cast in plaster wearing my favourite corduroy trousers, and will lie in state right in the centre of this room, never to leave again."

Beim Betreten von Peter Hones außergewöhnlicher Wohnung im Westen Londons wird man von Mr. Brown begrüßt, einem enthusiastischen Jack-Russell-Terrier – und vom Duft hausgemachten Chutneys, der aus der Küche strömt und an herbstliche Tage denken lässt. Hone wurde ursprünglich als Koch ausgebildet. Heute macht es ihm aber am meisten Spaß, auf jeder nur vorstellbaren Fläche seine »Sammlung des organisierten Chaos«, wie er sie selbst nennt, zu erweitern. Selbst die Decken werden bald mit unbezahlbarem und kunstvoll gearbeitetem Stuck bedeckt sein. Die neutralen Steinfarben schaffen ein Umfeld, das wie ein Traum wirkt, so, als würde man über einem Korallengarten schweben, in dem jedes Stück einzigartig ist, aber die Landschaft als Ganzes wahrgenommen wird. Das Himmelbett wäre der beste Aussichtspunkt auf die Schätze von Peter Hone. Bei der Frage, wie man mit dieser Sammlung wohl umziehen würde, überlegt der Hausherr und sagt: »Niemals! Ich werde dann auch in Gips gegossen, mit meinen Lieblingscordhosen, werde mitten in diesem Zimmer aufgebahrt und es nie wieder verlassen.«

Left: an 18th-century portrait of Thomas Oldknow by Joseph Wright of Derby.

A gauche: un portrait datant du 18ᵉ siècle de Thomas Oldknow par Joseph Wright of Derby.

Links: ein aus dem 18. Jahrhundert stammendes Porträt von Thomas Oldknow, gemalt von Joseph Wright of Derby.

Right: Peter Hone sitting on a plaster copy of Gianlorenzo Bernini's throne of Saint Peter, surrounded by his "spectacular array of Coade stone fragments, keystones, urns and sarcophagi"!

A droite: Peter Hone assis sur une copie en plâtre du trône de saint Pierre par Gianlorenzo Bernini, entouré d'un «spectaculaire assortiment de fragments, de clés de voûte, d'urnes et de sarcophages en pierre de Coade»!

Rechts: Peter Hone sitzt auf einer Gipsversion von Gianlorenzo Berninis Thron im Petersdom, umgeben von seiner »atemberaubenden Sammlung aus Coadestone-Fragmenten, Schlußsteinen, Urnen und Sarkophagen«!

Right: a first-century Greek marble carving of the head of Midas above a plaster hand, a copy of one at The British Museum.

A droite: une sculpture grecque datant du 1ᵉʳ siècle représentant le roi Midas, au-dessus d'une main en plâtre, copie d'un original conservé au British Museum.

Rechts: Ein aus dem 1. Jahrhundert stammender griechischer Marmorkopf des Midas, darüber eine Hand aus Gips, eine Kopie nach dem Original aus dem Britischen Museum.

Left: a statue of Flora by Antonio Canova (1757–1822) and, in the foreground, a head of Dr Samuel Johnson (1709–1784).

A gauche: une statue de Flora par Antonio Canova (1757–1822). Au premier plan, la tête du docteur Samuel Johnson (1709–1784).

Links: eine Statue der Flora von Antonio Canova (1757–1822). Im Vordergrund ein Kopf von Dr. Samuel Johnson (1709–1784).

Left: The fireplace, which is original to the building.

A gauche: La cheminée qui date de la construction de la maison.

Links: Der Kamin gehörte zur Originalausstattung des Hauses.

Left: Hone designed the chair standing in front of a 1930s Odeonesque alabaster vase.

A gauche: Hone a dessiné lui-même le fauteuil placé devant un vase en albâtre des années 1930 évoquant l'odéon.

Links: Der Stuhl ist ein Entwurf von Peter Hone. Dahinter steht eine Alabastervase, die griechisch-römisch wirkt, aber aus den 1930er Jahren stammt.

Right: Architectural fragments and an 1832 Coade stone hawk are displayed on a table from Castle Howard made by the estate carpenter.

A droite: des ornements architecturaux et un faucon en pierre de Coade, datant de 1832, placés sur une table provenant de Castle Howard et réalisée par le menuisier du domaine.

Rechts: Architekturfragmente und ein Falke aus Coadestone aus dem Jahr 1832 prunken auf einem Tisch aus Castle Howard, angefertigt vom dortigen Zimmermann.

Left: A plaster figure of the Duchess of Devonshire by Lucius Gahagan, dated 1830, sits on a turn-of-the-century servants' table.

A gauche: un buste en plâtre de la duchesse de Devonshire par Lucius Gahagan, daté 1830, sur une table de communs du début du siècle.

Links: Eine Gipsfigur der Herzogin von Devonshire von Lucius Gahagan aus dem Jahr 1830 steht auf einem Tisch aus der Zeit der Jahrhundertwende.

Left: a 1689 Queen Anne chair in front of a Coade stone urn on a marble table.

A gauche: un fauteuil Queen Anne de 1689 devant une urne en pierre de Coade posée sur un autel de thermes en marbre.

Links: ein Queen-Anne-Armlehnstuhl von 1689 vor einer Urne aus Coadestone auf einem Marmortisch.

Right: A Regency glass lantern hangs in the hall next to an early 18th-century cupboard.
Below: Above the doorway to the kitchen hangs a plaster frieze rescued from a former Paddington Green vicarage undergoing demolition. The paper "trompe l'œil" column is a copy of the 1790s original.

A droite: une lanterne Regency en verre, suspendue dans l'entrée près d'une armoire du début du 18e siècle.
Ci-dessous: au-dessus de la porte donnant sur la cuisine, un bas-relief en plâtre récupéré lors de la démolition d'un presbytère de Paddington Green. La colonne en trompe-l'œil est une copie d'un papier peint des années 1790.

Rechts: Im Flur hängt eine Glaslaterne aus der Zeit des Regency neben einem Schrank aus dem frühen 18. Jahrhundert.
Unten: Über der Küchentür fällt ein Gipsfries auf, der beim Abbruch eines Pfarrhauses in Paddington gerettet werden konnte. Die Trompel'œil-Säule aus Papier ist eine Kopie nach einem Original aus den 90er Jahren des 18. Jahrhunderts.

Above: Cut-out coronets from royal standards decorate the dark pink blinds. The rare Roman 2nd-century hippocampus (a mythical sea horse with a dolphin's tail), originally from Hadrian's villa but now resplendent in the centre of the window, was a fortunate discovery in a house sale of garden sculpture.
Right: An elegant 18th-century bed with fabric designed by John Fowler for Lady Anne Tree dominates the living room, providing a second bedroom when necessary.

Ci-dessus: Des couronnes découpées dans des bannières royales ornent les stores rose foncé. Devant la fenêtre, l'hippocampe mythique romain du 2ᵉ siècle, une pièce rare représentant un cheval marin avec une queue de dauphin, provient de la villa d'Hadrien. Hone est tombé dessus par hasard lors d'une vente privée de statues de jardin.
A droite: Un élégant lit à baldaquin du 18ᵉ siècle, tapissé d'un tissu créé par John Fowler pour Lady Anne Tree, domine le salon, servant de lit d'appoint pour les amis.

Oben: Ausgeschnitten aus königlichen Standarten sind die Kronen, die die pinkfarbenen Rollos schmücken. Direkt vor dem Fenster steht ein seltener römischer Hippocampus aus dem 2. Jahrhundert; das mythische Seepferd mit Delfinschwanz stammt aus der Hadrian-Villa und war ein Glücksfund bei einem Privatverkauf von Gartenskulpturen.
Rechts: Ein elegantes Bett aus dem 18. Jahrhundert dominiert das Wohnzimmer, das bei Bedarf zum zweiten Schlafzimmer wird. John Fowler entwarf den Stoff für Lady Anne Tree.

Lorsque les peintres Georgie Hopton et Gary Hume, membres du courant des Young British Artists, se sont rencontrés, ce dernier squattait une remise en briques, sans chauffage ni eau chaude, dans un coin délabré de l'est londonien. Le lit n'était qu'un grand matelas posé à même le sol, sous une tente fixée à un mur et entourée de ses œuvres. Même si l'espace était grand et très lumineux, idéal pour peindre, Hume reconnaît aujourd'hui que «c'était franchement sordide». Hopton ne pouvait envisager leur avenir ensemble sans, au moins, une baignoire. Sept ans plus tard, Hoxton est devenu le quartier branché, Hopton a épousé Hume, et un grand tub en fonte domine désormais la salle de bains. D'autres aménagements bassement matériels ont été ajoutés, tels qu'un réfrigérateur, des chambres et même un toit étanche. Ayant rendu l'espace habitable, Georgie Hopton a entrepris de le rendre beau, ajoutant ici et là des touches nettement féminines.

Gary Hume & Georgie Hopton

When painters Gary Hume and Georgie Hopton met, he was squatting in a brick shed in Hoxton, then a grotty corner of East London. The squat had no heating or hot water and his bed was just a double mattress on the floor, inside a tent pitched at one end of the room, surrounded by his paintings. Even though the shed was huge and light-filled – perfect for painting – it was "pretty revolting", Hume now admits. Hopton couldn't see how they could have a future together if they didn't even have a bath. Seven years on, Hoxton has become trendy, Hopton has married Hume, a vast cast-iron tub dominates the bathroom, and other creature comforts – including a fridge, bedrooms and even a rainproof roof – have been added. Having made the former squat habitable in a practical sense, Hopton set about transforming the look of the space, adding her own distinctly feminine flourishes.

Als sich die Maler Gary Hume und Georgie Hopton aus der Gruppe der Young British Artists kennenlernten, lebte Gary Hume als Hausbesetzer in diesem Backsteinschuppen in einer damals heruntergekommenen Gegend im Osten Londons. Heizung und warmes Wasser gab es nicht. Als Bett diente eine Doppelmatratze auf dem Boden in einem Zelt, das in einer Ecke des Zimmers aufgestellt war. So war er umgeben von seinen Bildern. Der Raum war riesig und lichtdurchflutet und eignete sich perfekt als Atelier. Allerdings: »Es war auch ziemlich eklig«, gibt er heute zu. Georgie Hopton zumindest wusste nicht, wie sich eine gemeinsame Zukunft ohne ein Badezimmer gestalten sollte. Sieben Jahre später ist Hoxton zum In-Stadtteil geworden, Hopton und Hume haben geheiratet, eine riesige gusseiserne Badewanne beherrscht das Badezimmer, und auch anderer Luxus in Form von Kühlschrank und Schlafzimmern hat Einzug gehalten. Selbst durch das Dach regnet es nicht mehr rein. Nun, nachdem es sich hier leben lässt, widmet sich Georgie Hopton der Gestaltung des riesigen Raums und verleiht ihm einen unverkennbar femininen Touch.

Above: Using Hume's trademark household gloss paints, Hopton transformed his brown kitchen table while he was away. Kitchen paraphernalia fills the 1950s cupboard, which stands next to a turquoise door, leading to the studio. The sofa is covered in shocking pink velvet, the coffee table, whose simple design Hume admits to liking, is 1970s Perspex.
Right: The painted saw in the kitchen is a souvenir from Texas.
Facing page: The walls of the main living space are covered in work by Hume, Hopton and their friends, fellow Young British Artists.

Ci-dessus: Hopton a profité d'une absence de Hume pour transformer sa table de cuisine brune à l'aide des peintures murales satinées qu'il utilise pour son art. Près d'une porte turquoise donnant sur l'atelier, le meuble des années 1950 est rempli d'ustensiles de cuisine. Le sofa est tapissé de velours rose bonbon. Hume admet qu'il a un faible pour les lignes simples de la table basse en Perspex des années 1970.
A droite: La scie peinte dans la cuisine est un souvenir du Texas.
Page de droite: Les murs de l'espace de séjour sont tapissés d'œuvres de Hume, de Hopton et de leurs amis, également membres du courant des Young British Artists.

Oben: Während Gary Humes Abwesenheit machte Georgie Hopton aus seinem braunem Tisch etwas ganz Neues, verwendete dabei allerdings die für ihn typischen Haushaltslacke. Die Küchengeräte werden in dem Schrank aus den 1950er Jahren aufbewahrt, der neben der Tür steht, die zum Atelier führt. Das Sofa ist mit Samt in Knallpink bezogen; Hume dagegen bekennt sich zu seiner Vorliebe für das einfache Design des Perspex-Couchtischs aus den 1970er Jahren.
Rechts: Die bemalte Säge in der Küche ist ein Souvenir aus Texas.
Rechte Seite: An den Wänden des Wohnraums hängen Arbeiten von Hume, Hopton und ihren Künstlerfreunden aus der Gruppe der Young British Artists.

Le terme «éclectique» est terriblement galvaudé dans le monde de la décoration d'intérieur, mais parfois c'est le seul qui puisse traduire succinctement l'esprit d'une maison et, dans le cas présent, aucun autre mot ne saura mieux décrire celui de cette bâtisse classique de Notting Hill, construite en 1856, où vivent Judy Kleinman et son mari Daniel, réalisateur de longs métrages et de publicités. «Je ne voulais pas qu'on entre chez moi en disant: «Oh! Comme c'est victorien» ou «Que c'est moderne!», explique Judy. Si, tout au long des années 1990, les intérieurs typiques étaient empreints d'un minimalisme dépouillé agrémenté de quelques touches modernistes, la fin de la décennie a vu fleurir des styles «pots pourris» plus nuancés, reflétant l'apparente confusion fin de siècle de la mode. Toutefois, plutôt qu'une forme d'insécurité collective, cette nouvelle tendance annonce le retour bienvenu des styles personnels bien assumés. En évitant délibérément un look «de décorateur», Judy Kleinman a créé sans le savoir l'incarnation même du style du tournant du nouveau millénaire.

Judy Kleinman

"Eclectic" is a word so overused in designer-speak that it is in danger of becoming a cliché. But sometimes there is only word that succinctly captures the feeling of a home and, in this instance, "eclectic" it must be. "The overriding thing was that I didn't want anyone to be able to walk in and just say: 'Oh, it's Victorian' or 'It's modern'", explains Judy Kleinman, who lives in this classic Notting Hill house, built in 1856, with her film and advertising director husband Daniel. While cutting-edge 1990s interiors were all bare minimalism with modernist flourishes, the beginning of the new century sees a trend towards a softer, anything-goes potpourri of styles, echoing fashion's apparent millennial confusion. But rather than a form of collective insecurity, this new mood heralds a welcome return of confidence in individual style. By determinedly avoiding a designer look, Judy Kleinman has inadvertently created a home that is the embodiment of style at the turn of the millennium.

Der Begriff »Stilmix« wird in der Sprache der Designer so oft verwendet, dass daraus schon ein Klischee zu werden droht. Doch manchmal trifft diese Beschreibung haargenau zu – wie bei diesem Haus. »Am allerwichtigsten war mir, dass niemand in das Haus kommen könnte und gleich sagen würde, ›Ah, Ihr habt es viktorianisch‹ oder ›Ihr seid modern eingerichtet‹«, erklärt Judy Kleinman. Sie lebt in diesem für Notting Hill typischen Haus aus dem Jahr 1856 gemeinsam mit ihrem Mann Daniel, der Filme macht und in der Werbeindustrie tätig ist. Während die heißesten Trends der 1990er Jahre vom puren Minimalismus mit modernistischen Anklängen lebten, kündigt sich nun eine Entwicklung zu einem sanfteren Stil an, in dem Verschiedenes wie ein Potpourri gemixt werden kann und alles erlaubt ist – vergleichbar der Millennium-Konfusion in der Modewelt. Doch aus dieser neuen Stimmung entwickelt sich keine Form der kollektiven Unsicherheit. Vielmehr signalisiert sie die äußerst willkommene Rückkehr des individuellen Stils. Durch das ganz bewusste Vermeiden eines Designlooks hat Judy Kleinman fast versehentlich ein Zuhause geschaffen, das den Stil zur Millenniumswende verkörpert.

Right: The elegant joinery by Milka Jvestica creates continuity between the dining area and compact kitchen. Only the essentials are on display, the microwave and fridge being hidden away in an understair pantry. The Kleinmans and their friends lovingly created the Italian marble mosaic floor over eight months. Each made their own interpretation of "a long-necked bird", which Judy painstakingly joined together in swirls of buff-coloured mosaic.
Below: In a window recess on the basement level, a Lounge Chair and ottoman, designed by Charles Eames in 1956, are irreverently covered in fake tiger fur.

A droite: L'élégante menuiserie de Milka Jvestica assure une continuité entre le coin salle à manger et la toute petite cuisine. On ne voit que l'essentiel. Le four à micro-ondes et le réfrigérateur sont cachés dans l'office, lui-même caché sous l'escalier. Les Kleinman et leurs amis ont mis huit mois à créer avec amour le sol en mosaïque de marbres italiens. Chacun a interprété à sa manière un «oiseau au long cou»; Judy les a ensuite minutieusement reliés avec de la mosaïque couleur chamois.
Ci-dessous: Dans un renfoncement de la fenêtre au sous-sol, un fauteuil et un repose-pied, dessinés par Eames en 1956, sont tapissés avec humour de faux tigre.

Rechts: Die eleganten Schreinerarbeiten von Milka Jvestica verbinden Essbereich und Kompaktküche. Nur das Allernotwendigste ist sichtbar; Mikrowelle und Kühlschrank sind in der Speisekammer unter der Treppe versteckt. Mit viel Liebe haben die Kleinmans und ihre Freunde in acht Monaten den italienischen Mosaikboden aus Marmor verlegt. Jeder schuf seine eigene Interpretation eines »Vogels mit langem Hals«, und Judy bettete sie alle sorgfältig zwischen gelbbraune Mosaiksteinchen ein.
Unten: In einem Erker im Souterrain steht ein Lounge Chair mit passender Ottomane, von Charles Eames 1956 entworfen und hier respektlos mit Tigerfellstoff bezogen.

Above: Layers of cream gloss on sanded and filled maple floorboards add a sleek textural element to the basement kitchen and dining level. The warm tone of the pale green walls, which changes with the light throughout the day, is a perfect backdrop for the Kleinmans' diverse collection of furniture. The black marble dining table is Florence Knoll; the dining chairs are American 1960s.
Right: A silk and gilt Chinese tapestry hangs unexpectedly above the state-of-the-art industrial stainless-steel cooker in a wall recess of the kitchen area.

Ci-dessus: Des couches de peinture crème satinée sur le parquet en érable aux jointures comblées donnent une allure lisse au coin salle à manger et cuisine du sous-sol. Le ton chaleureux des murs vert pâle, qui change au fil du jour, offre une toile de fond idéale à la collection bigarrée de meubles des Kleinman. La table en marbre noire est de Florence Knoll; les chaises des années 1960 sont américaines.
A droite: Détail inattendu, dans un recoin de la cuisine, une tenture chinoise en soie et fils d'or est suspendue au-dessus de l'ultramoderne cuisinière industrielle en acier.

Oben: Der in Schichten aufgetragene, eierschalenfarbene Gloss auf den abgezogenen und ausgefugten Dielenböden aus Ahorn verleiht dem im Souterrain gelegenen Koch- und Essbereich Eleganz. Die blassgrünen Wände, deren warmer Farbton sich im Laufe des Tages mit dem Lichteinfall verändert, bilden den perfekten Hintergrund für die breitgefächerte Möbelsammlung der Kleinmans. Der schwarze Esstisch aus Marmor stammt von Florence Knoll, die Stühle aus dem Amerika der 1960er Jahre.
Rechts: In einer Nische in der Küche überrascht ein chinesischer Gobelin aus Seide und Gold über einem ultramodernen Profiherd aus rostfreiem Edelstahl.

Brick Lane, London E1

De nos jours, les lofts en ville sont restaurés à grands frais et vendus à prix d'or par les agents immobiliers qui les présentent comme le choix idéal pour vivre avec son temps. Leur attrait repose en partie sur l'image, née au début des années 1990, d'artistes s'appropriant des bâtiments vides et délabrés du centre-ville parce qu'ils étaient spacieux, bien éclairés, et, surtout, bon marché. Les artistes Michael Landy et Gillian Wearing ont emménagé au dernier étage d'un immeuble délabré de Brick Lane il y a trois ans parce qu'il leur fallait un endroit pour vivre et travailler et que c'était là l'option la moins coûteuse. Avec le recul, ils reconnaissent qu'un tel espace, avec ses 185 mètres carrés habitables plus 95 autres en terrasse, est presque trop grand. Le couple a cloisonné un coin du loft pour se créer une chambre et lui donner un aspect plus «maison», tandis que Landy a utilisé les fameuses caisses dont il se sert pour son art pour définir des petits coins intimes. «Dans notre prochain appartement», confie-t-il, «j'aimerais bien avoir des portes et des murs».

Michael Landy & Gillian Wearing

Today, urban lofts are expensively packaged and marketed by estate agents as the modern lifestyle choice. In the early 1990s, artists chose these often empty, run-down, inner city buildings because they were large, light and – most importantly – cheap. Artists Michael Landy and Gillian Wearing moved into their dilapidated top-floor space near Brick Lane three years ago because they needed somewhere to work and live and this was the cheapest option. Today it is prime real estate. On reflection, Landy admits to finding such a large space – 2,000 square feet inside and another 1,000 on the terrace – almost too big. The couple partitioned off a corner to create a bedroom and make the spacious loft feel like a home. Landy has used his trademark crates to make more defined and intimate areas. "In the next place I think I will want walls and doors," he says.

Heutzutage preisen Makler Lofts als Inbegriff modernen Wohn- und Lebensstils an und verkaufen sie entsprechend teuer. Die Attraktivität von Lofts beruht zum Teil darauf, dass Künstler, die Anfang der 1990er Jahre leer stehenden und heruntergekommenen Gebäude im Stadtzentrum übernahmen, weil sie groß, hell und – der wichtigste Aspekt – günstig waren. Die Künstler Michael Landy und Gillian Wearing zogen vor drei Jahren in das oberste Stockwerk eines vom Verfall bedrohten Gebäudes nahe Brick Lane, weil sie einen Platz zum Arbeiten und Leben brauchten und dies die billigste Alternative war. Bei näherer Betrachtung muss Michael Landy allerdings zugeben, dass er einen so großen Raum – 185 Quadratmeter im Innenbereich und weitere knapp 95 Quadratmeter als Terrasse – fast schon zu groß findet. Einen Teil trennte sich das Paar als Schlafzimmer ab. Um für klare Linien und mehr Intimität zu sorgen, hat Michael Landy den Raum mit seinen charakteristischen Stapelboxen unterteilt. »Aber in der nächsten Wohnung möchte ich Türen und Wände«, sagt er.

Previous page: Michael, Gillian and Rat-a-kins, who was discovered at Battersea Dogs Home, which also rescues unwanted cats.
Right: Wearing's work den is also the couple's bedroom, where in winter she spends most of her time on the Internet with electric radiators to keep her warm. The wooden stage is a reminder of the space's former life as a dance club, before which it had been a sweatshop.
Below: Landy's personalised crates act as movable walls, allowing the space to be constantly reconfigured. On a "wall" hangs one of his intricate working drawings.

Page précédente : Michael, Gillian et Rat-a-kins, découvert au refuge pour chiens de Battersea, qui recueille également les chats.
A droite : L'espace de travail de Wearing est également la chambre à coucher du couple. L'hiver, elle passe le plus clair de son temps ici à surfer sur Internet, à la chaleur des radiateurs électriques. L'estrade en bois est un souvenir de la précédente incarnation des lieux, un club de danse. Auparavant, il y avait un atelier de confection.
Ci-dessous : Les caisses personnalisées de Landing servent de murs amovibles, permettant de remodeler sans cesse l'espace. Sur l'un des «murs», un de ses complexes dessins de travail.

Vorhergehende Seite: Michael, Gillian und Rat-a-kins. Das Paar fand Rat-a-kins im Battersea Dogs Home, das auch Katzen aufnimmt.
Rechts: Wearings Arbeitszimmer ist gleichzeitig das gemeinsame Schlafzimmer. Im Winter verbringt sie die meiste Zeit hier – beim Internetsurfen und umgeben von elektrischen Heizkörpern, um sich warm zu halten. Die Holzbühne erinnert daran, dass das Loft früher ein »dance club« war. Und davor wurde hier im Akkord genäht.
Unten: Landy »personalisierte« nüchterne Stapelboxen und nutzt sie als bewegliche Wände, um den Raum immer wieder neu zu gestalten. An einer »Wand« hängt eine seiner detaillierten Arbeitsskizzen.

Above: The crates evolved out of Landy's work at the beginning of the 1990s, which looked at how market vendors use bread crates to make impermanent display structures. His early installations used crates from Allied Bakeries, but these later ones were produced with his name stamped on them.

Right: The bed is in the corner of Wearing's workroom under the gas meter. Landy built a plasterboard wall to separate off this area, so that he "wouldn't have to wake up and see the whole space," he explains.

Ci-dessus: L'idée de travailler avec des caisses est venue à Landing au début des années 1990, quand il s'est intéressé à la manière dont les vendeurs sur les marchés les utilisaient pour se confectionner des étals de fortune. Pour ses premières installations, il s'est servi de caisses des «Boulangers réunis». A présent, celles qu'il utilise sont estampillées de son nom.

A droite: Le lit occupe un angle de l'atelier de Wearing, sous le compteur à gaz. Landing a monté une cloison au placoplâtre afin d'isoler ce coin et «ne pas avoir à se réveiller en voyant tout l'espace.»

Oben: Seine Arbeiten aus Stapelboxen entwickelten sich zu Beginn der 1990er Jahre, als sich Landy bei Marktverkäufern abguckte, wie man aus Transportkästen für Brot Marktstände gestalten konnte. Für seine ersten Installationen verwendete er noch Kisten von Allied Bakeries; die hier abgebildeten Boxen wurden später produziert und tragen bereits aufgedruckt seinen Namen.

Rechts: Das Bett steht in der Ecke von Wearings Arbeitsraum, direkt unter dem Gaszähler. Landy zog eine Wand aus Gipskarton ein, »um nicht morgens gleich beim Aufwachen den ganzen Raum sehen zu müssen«.

Facing page: Landy laid the cork tiles on the floor when they moved in. A cosy area has been partitioned off in the centre of the space using Landy's crates. The soft fluffy blanket on the sofa was bought for 25 pounds from a shop in nearby Brick Lane.
Above: The top-floor space has windows across three sides, making it gloriously light even on a dull day, but wretchedly cold in winter. The building is right next to an imposing 18th-century church by Nicholas Hawksmoor and there are panoramic views from the terrace of the City's landmark buildings.

Page de droite: Landing a posé le sol en plaques de liège lorsqu'ils ont emménagé. Un petit coin douillet a été isolé au centre du loft à l'aide des caisses de Landing. La couverture pelucheuse sur le canapé a été achetée 25 livres dans une boutique voisine sur Brick Lane.
Ci-dessus: Situé au dernier étage, le loft a des fenêtres sur trois côtés, ce qui le rend inondé de lumière même les jours les plus mornes, mais également glacial en hiver. L'immeuble jouxte une imposante église construite par Nicholas Hawksmoor au 18ᵉ siècle et, de la terrasse, on a une vue panoramique sur les grands monuments de la capitale.

Rechte Seite: Beim Einzug verlegte Michael Landy Korkfliesen auf dem Boden. Mitten im Raum entstand hinter Stapelboxen eine Kuschelecke. Die weiche Plüschdecke auf dem Sofa wurde für wenig Geld in einem Laden in der Brick Lane erworben.
Oben: Das oberste Stockwerk ist an drei Seiten verglast, sodass es selbst an trüben Tagen hier wunderbar hell ist, im Winter allerdings auch eisig kalt. Das Gebäude steht neben einer imposanten Kirche von Nicholas Hawksmoor aus dem 18. Jahrhundert, und die Terrasse bietet einen Panoramablick auf die bekanntesten Gebäude der City.

Cette maison à Hampstead, datant des années 1730 et unique en son genre, a connu une destinée haute en couleurs. Après avoir été la demeure du peintre George Romney (1734–1802), elle a accueilli la «Société conservatrice de Hamsptead», avant de devenir aujourd'hui la maison de famille de Nick et de Maxine Leslau. Sa façade en bois et briques rappelant davantage la Nouvelle- Angleterre que le nord de Londres, il n'est pas étonnant qu'elle ait séduit Maxine, arrivée des Etats-Unis il y a une quinzaine d'années. Classée monument historique, on ne peut pas toucher à l'extérieur du bâtiment, mais les mêmes restrictions ne s'appliquent pas à l'intérieur. Maxine a utilisé un mobilier et des tissus d'ameublement capables de résister aux mauvais traitements de ses trois fils. Derrière l'harmonie de couleur café et crème, la plupart des meubles sont bon marché et tous sont recouverts de housses lavables. La pièce la plus impressionnante est l'ancien atelier de Romney, si grande que Maxine l'appelle la «salle de bal». «Tout est à l'échelle d'Alice au pays des merveilles» confie-t-elle.

Nick & Maxine Leslau

This unique 1730s Hampstead house has had a varied life, at one time as the home of the painter George Romney (1734–1802), later of the Hampstead Conservative Society, and today of Nick and Maxine Leslau and their family. The clapboard and brick construction is more New England than north London, so it's not surprising that Maxine, who arrived from the States over 15 years ago, was attracted to it. As a grade one listed building, the exterior has to remain unchanged, but the same restrictions do not apply to the interior. Maxine used furnishings that could take the wear and tear of her three boys, so even though the decor is a harmony of coffee and cream, many pieces are inexpensive, and everything has removable covers. The most impressive room was formerly Romney's studio, which Maxine jokingly refers to as the "ballroom" because it is so large. "Everything is Alice-in-Wonderland scale," she says. The boys find it great for roller skating too.

Dieses außergewöhnliche, um 1730 erbaute Haus in Hampstead birgt eine abwechslungsreiche Geschichte: Erst lebte und malte hier George Romney (1734–1802), dann war es die Adresse der Hampstead Conservative Society, und heute ist es das Zuhause von Nick und Maxine Leslau und ihrer Familie. Der Baustil – Schindeln und Backstein – erinnert eher an Neuengland als an Nord-London. Es überrascht also kaum, dass Maxine Leslau, die vor mehr als 15 Jahren aus den Vereinigten Staaten kam, das Haus sofort mochte. Da es unter Denkmalschutz steht, dürfen an der Fassade keinerlei Eingriffe vorgenommen werden; diese Einschränkung gilt allerdings nicht für den Innenbereich. Die Möbel wurden mit Blick auf ihre Belastbarkeit ausgewählt – das Paar hat drei Jungen –, und obwohl der Gesamteindruck der einer stilvollen Melange aus Kaffee- und Sahnetönen ist, sind die meisten Stücke nicht teuer und mit abnehmbaren Bezügen kindersicher ausgestattet. Der eindrucksvollste Raum des Hauses war früher das Studio des Malers Romney. Wegen seiner Größe nennt ihn Maxine den »Ballsaal«. »Alles hat Dimensionen wie in ›Alice im Wunderland‹.« Und eignet sich zudem bestens zum Rollschuhlaufen.

Clockwise from top left: *The floor in the entrance porch is in the original marble; Maxine has converted two old metal fridges into bedside tables in the master bedroom; to the left of the entrance hall is a narrow staircase that leads to a hidden passage connected to "the ballroom"; overscaled chairs by Orianna Fielding Banks encircle a table with a base made from French wrought-iron balconies.*

Du haut à gauche, dans le sens des aiguilles d'une montre: *Le sol à damier du porche d'entrée a gardé ses marbres d'origine; Maxine a transformé deux vieux réfrigérateurs en tables de chevet; sur la gauche*

du vestibule, un escalier étroit mène vers une galerie secrète reliée à la «salle de bal»; des chaises d'Oriana Fielding Banks encerclent une table dont la base a été créée avec des balustrades de balcons.

Im Uhrzeigersinn von links oben: *Der Marmorboden im Eingangsbereich ist original; zwei alte Metallkühlschränke wurden von Maxine Leslau zu Nachtschränkchen umfunktioniert; links führt eine schmale Treppe von der Eingangshalle zu einem Geheimweg, der mit dem »Ballsaal« verbunden ist; die Stühle sind von Orianna Fielding Banks. Der Fuß des Tischs besteht aus gusseisernen Balkongittern.*

London Interiors   Nick & Maxine Leslau

Clockwise from top left: *The bath is set into a "beach"; John Paw-son's minimal architecture was the inspiration for the pedestal sink; doors lead onto the roof, where Maxine has a small studio and can enjoy views across London to St Paul's Cathedral; a painting in the bedroom was commissioned from Jean-Paul Philippe and is an abstraction of Maxine's and her husband Nick's initials.*

Du haut à gauche, dans le sens des aiguilles d'une montre: *La baignoire est enchâssée dans une «plage»; l'architecture minimaliste de John Pawson a servi d'inspiration pour ce lavabo; les portes donnent*

sur le toit où Maxine s'est installé un petit atelier et d'où l'on voit tout Londres; dans la chambre, un tableau de Jean-Paul Philippe et représentant une abstraction des initiales de Maxine et de Nick.

Im Uhrzeigersinn von links oben: *Die Wanne ist in einen »Strand« eingelassen; John Pawsons minimalistische Architektur stand Pate für das Waschbecken; die Tür führt zum Dach, wo Maxine Leslau ihr eigenes Studio mit Blick über ganz London besitzt; das Bild im Schlafzimmer von Jean-Paul Philippe zeigt eine abstrakte Interpretation der Initialen des Ehepaars.*

Il y a trois ans, Tom et Polly Lloyd ont décidé qu'ils en avaient assez du West End, trop cher et trop branché. Ils y ont tous les deux grandi mais se sont rencontrés pendant leurs études à Nottingham. Ces dix dernières années, ils ont vu leur quartier de Notting Hill, autrefois funky et rempli de vrais artistes, devenir une enclave de boutiques chic et aseptisées aux allures faussement bohèmes. Les Lloyd ont alors décidé de fuir vers l'est, troquant leur petit appartement contre ce grand bâtiment industriel de l'ère victorienne au cœur d'Hackney. Au cours de ses vies antérieures, la bâtisse a accueilli un atelier d'imprimerie et une fabrique de pianos. Les fenêtres métalliques rouillées ont été remplacées, le parquet a été laborieusement poncé pour ôter des années de crasse, les murs ont été enduits au plâtre là où c'était nécessaire. Le résultat : une maison de trois étages avec un jardin, un coin bureau, un espace atelier et une terrasse sur le toit qui est presque achevée. Il y a toutefois un hic : Hackney est en passe de devenir le quartier le plus branché de la capitale !

Tom & Polly Lloyd

Tom and Polly Lloyd decided they'd had enough of overpriced and overhyped West London three years ago. The couple grew up in that area, but met while studying in Nottingham. In the intervening decade or so they watched their local neighbourhood, Notting Hill, change from genuinely funky and artistic to the commercially homogenised and self-consciously bohemian enclave it is today. The Lloyds decided to move east, exchanging a modest flat for this large Victorian commercial building in Hackney. In previous incarnations the building had been a printing workshop and a piano factory. Crumbling metal windows were replaced; years of grime were painstakingly removed from the wood floorboards; walls were replastered where necessary, left natural when possible. The result is a three-story home with courtyard garden, office and studio space, and a roof terrace nearing completion. The only irony – Hackney is fast becoming the coolest borough in town.

Vor drei Jahren waren Tom und Polly Lloyd des Londoner Westens, der immer angesagter und teurer wurde, endgültig überdrüssig. Beide waren hier aufgewachsen, hatten sich allerdings während des Studiums in Nottingham kennen gelernt. Im Jahrzehnt dazwischen wurden sie Zeugen, wie »ihr« Stadtteil Notting Hill mit seinem abgerockten, authentischen und auf Kunst ausgerichteten Leben abschloss und sich zur kommerziellen Enklave einer scheinbaren Boheme entwickelte. Das Paar beschloss, gen Osten zu ziehen und tauschte seine bescheidene Wohnung in Notting Hill gegen ein riesiges Gebäude aus viktorianischer Zeit im Herzen von Hackney. In seinen früheren Leben war es mal Druckerei und mal Klavierfabrik. Die verrosteten Metallfenster wurden ersetzt, jahrzehntealter Industrieschmutz sorgfältig vom Holzboden entfernt und Wände neu vergipst oder – wo das möglich war – roh belassen. Das Ergebnis ist ein dreistöckiges Haus mit einem nach hinten liegenden Garten, einem Büro, einem Designstudio und bald auch einer Dachterrasse. Doch leider entbehrt die ganze Mühe nicht einer gewissen Ironie: Mittlerweile entwickelt sich nämlich ausgerechnet Hackney zum angesagtesten Stadtteil Londons!

Previous page: Smooth, freshly plastered ceilings abut walls of distressed brickwork and peeling paint. Eero Saarinen's "Tulip" chairs dating from 1955/56, a home and office storage unit designed by Tom Lloyd for Knoll and a rough wood table also create a pleasing contrast of textures.

Right and below: On the first floor, the L-shaped living space has a kitchen that combines rustic simplicity with modern essentials. Storage shelves left behind by the print workshop are now filled with crockery and cooking equipment. The chrome and leather "B33" chairs were designed by Marcel Breuer in 1927/28.

Page précédente: Les plafonds fraîchement plâtrés jouxtent des murs de briques nues et des vestiges de peinture. Les chaises «Tulip» d'Eero Saarinen datant de 1955/56, un meuble de rangement pour bureau dessiné par Tom Lloyd pour Knoll et une table en bois brut créent également un agréable contraste de textures.

A droite et ci-dessous: Au premier étage, la vaste salle de séjour en L est équipée d'une cuisine qui associe une simplicité rustique aux conforts modernes indispensables. Les étagères de l'ancien atelier d'imprimerie accueillent désormais des ustensiles de cuisine et la vaisselle. Les chaises en chrome et cuir «B33» ont été dessinées par Marcel Breuer en 1927/28.

Vorhergehende Seite: Frisch verputzte glatte Decken und Wände, denen man ihr geschundenes Innenleben aus Mauerwerk und abbröckelnder Farbe ansieht. Eero Saarinens Entwurf der »Tulip«-Stühle stammt von 1955/56. Das Aufbewahrungssystem für Büroräume entwarf Tom Lloyd für die Firma Knoll. Dazwischen sorgt ein nicht bearbeiteter Holztisch für interessante Texturkontraste.

Rechts und unten: Die Küche im L-förmig angelegten Wohnraum im ersten Stock vereint rustikale Einfachheit mit allem, was man heute braucht. In den noch aus Druckereizeiten stammenden Regalen werden Kochgeschirr und Utensilien aufbewahrt. Die »B33«-Stühle aus Chrom und Leder entwarf Marcel Breuer zwischen 1927 und 1928.

Above: A wood-burning stove heats the large open-plan living room, which is filled with a confident mix of traditional and contemporary furniture, including a "Diamond" chair by Harry Bertoia (1950–52) and an Eero Saarinen "Womb" chair (1947/48). An abstract knitted textile draped over the sofa was a wedding gift made by Polly's mother.
Right: A grand piano stands in front of French windows that lead to the courtyard garden below. The two acrylic paintings of seedpods above are by Tom's sister Olivia Lloyd.

Ci-dessus: La grande salle de séjour à plan ouvert est chauffée par un poêle à bois. Elle est meublée d'un bel assortiment de meubles traditionnels et contemporains, dont un fauteuil «Diamond» d'Harry Bertoia (1950–52) et d'une chaise «Womb» d'Eero Saarinen (1947/48). Sur le canapé, un plaid en tricot aux motifs abstraits, cadeau de mariage de la mère de Polly.
A droite: un piano à queue devant la baie vitrée qui donne sur la cour, aménagée en jardin. La sœur de Tom, Olivia Lloyd, a réalisé les peintures acryliques représentant des cosses de légumes.

Oben: Ein Holzofen beheizt den großen Wohnbereich ohne Trennwände. Traditionelle und moderne Möbel sind hier mit Selbstvertrauen gemixt, darunter Harry Bertoias »Diamond«-Sessel (1950–52) und Eero Saarinens »Womb«-Sessel (1947/48). Auf dem Sofa liegt ein Häkelüberwurf mit geometrischen Mustern – ein Hochzeitsgeschenk von Pollys Mutter.
Rechts: Vor den Balkontüren, durch die man in den darunter liegenden Innenhofgarten gelangt, steht ein Flügel. Die beiden Acrylbilder von Toms Schwester Olivia Lloyd stellen Samenstände dar.

Above: *Curtains separate the Lloyds' design studio and office area from the bedroom and bathroom on the second floor. The detritus of years of use as a print factory had to be laboriously scraped from the wood floors throughout the building.*
Right: *The bedroom has the luxury of overlooking treetops, belying the building's urban location. A Heal's 1930s cricket pavilion chair is used as a dressing stand and an old Turkish kilim rug covers some of the floorboards.*

Ci-dessus: *Au second étage, l'atelier de design et le bureau des Lloyd sont séparés de leur chambre à coucher et de leur salle de bains par des rideaux. Dans tout le bâtiment, il a fallu laborieusement poncer le plancher pour le débarrasser des années de crasse accumulées par l'atelier d'imprimerie.*
A droite: *Luxe suprême, les fenêtres de la chambre donnent sur des cimes d'arbres, si bien qu'on se croirait à la campagne. Un fauteuil de tribune de cricket des années 1930, de Heal's, sert de valet de nuit. Sur le parquet, un vieux kilim turc.*

Oben: *Designstudio und Büro der Lloyds sind durch Vorhänge vom Schlafzimmer und Bad im zweiten Stock abgetrennt. Der Schmutz, der sich über die Jahre in der Druckerei angesammelt hatte, musste sorgfältig von den Dielen entfernt werden, mit denen das ganze Gebäude ausgelegt ist.*
Rechts: *Das Schlafzimmer bietet den in der Stadt ungewöhnlichen Luxus, über die Baumwipfel hinweg blicken zu können. Von Heal's stammt der Stuhl aus den 1930er Jahren, der aus einem Cricketpavillon stammt und hier zum Stummen Diener geworden ist. Ein alter türkischer Kelim bedeckt die Dielen.*

London Interiors   Tom & Polly Lloyd

Clockwise from top left: the original factory doors leading onto the stairwell; two of Polly's collection of masks from Mali stand beside a small chest of drawers left behind by the print workshop; worn wood, paint and brickwork highlight the freshness of white towels in the bathroom; stair-treads worn down by many years of use.

Du haut à gauche, dans le sens des aiguilles d'une montre: Les anciennes portes de la fabrique donnent sur la cage d'escalier; deux des masques maliens de la collection de Polly, près d'une petite commode abandonnée par les imprimeurs; le bois usé, les briques et la peinture écaillée font ressortir la blancheur des serviettes dans la salle de bains; les marches de l'escaliers usées par des années de service.

Im Uhrzeigersinn von links oben: Die Originaltüren der einstigen Fabrik führen zum Treppenaufgang; zwei Masken aus Polly Lloyds Maskensammlung aus Mali stehen neben einer kleinen Kommode, die noch aus den Zeiten der Druckerei stammt; Holz mit Gebrauchsspuren, Farbe und Mauerwerk bringen die Frische der weißen Handtücher im Badezimmer zur Geltung; die Treppe ist durch jahrelange Nutzung abgetreten.

London Interiors   Tom & Polly Lloyd

At present, heavy cotton curtains are all that separate the bathroom from the bed and office areas on the second floor. The plan is to install sliding doors. A white partition wall to the left and the freshly plastered exterior wall opposite highlight the rich textures and subtle coloration of the facing wall.

Pour le moment, de lourds rideaux en coton séparent la salle de bains de la chambre et du bureau au second étage. Il est question de les remplacer par des portes coulissantes. Une cloison blanche et le mur extérieur fraîchement enduit au plâtre font ressortir les textures riches et les couleurs subtiles du troisième mur laissé en l'état.

Im Moment trennen nur schwere Baumwollvorhänge das Badezimmer von Schlafbereich und dem Bürobereich im zweiten Stock. Geplant ist der Einbau von Schiebetüren. Die weiße Trennwand links und die frisch vergipste Wand auf der gegenüberliegenden Außenseite betonen das Spektrum unterschiedlicher Texturen und die subtile Farbgebung der hinteren Wand.

Anciens camarades au Royal College of Art, le peintre Chris Ofili et
l'architecte David Adjaye se sont retrouvés lorsqu'Ofili a décidé de
transformer ce bâtiment victorien dans le East End en maison-atelier.
Bien qu'il soit souvent déconseillé de mélanger l'amitié et le travail,
Ofili en garde un excellent souvenir, déclarant même que «d'une certaine manière, travailler avec David m'a aidé à définir la façon dont je
voulais vivre». Ofili estimait important, tant pour lui-même que pour
ses amis de passage, de ne pas laisser son travail empiéter sur sa vie
privée. Deux espaces séparés mais reliés entre eux ont donc été créés.
Un atelier de peinture orienté vers le nord et un petit jardin occupent
la partie arrière du rez-de-chaussée, le côté rue étant réservé à l'espace
bureau et le sous-sol à l'atelier de dessin. Les autres étages au-dessus
constituent un lieu de vie ouvert.

Chris Ofili

Painter Chris Ofili and architect David Adjaye met at the Royal College of Art. Their friendship developed into a working relationship
when Ofili decided to convert this Victorian East End building into
a studio and home. While it's often advisable not to mix friendship
and work, Ofili says it was actually an enjoyable experience and explains that "in a way, the process of working with David helped me
define how I wanted to live here." Ofili felt it was important, both
for himself and for anyone staying at the house, to keep work away
from his private life, and the result is two separately defined but
connected spaces. A north-facing painting studio and small exterior terrace take up the back section of the ground floor, with an office area at the front and drawing studio in the basement. Above
are four floors of self-contained living space.

Auf dem Royal College of Art lernten sich der Maler Chris Ofili und
der Architekt David Adjaye kennen. Aus ihrer Freundschaft entwickelte sich eine berufliche Verbundenheit, nachdem Chris Ofili beschlossen hatte, dieses viktorianische Haus im Londoner East End in
eine Wohnung plus Atelier zu verwandeln. Nicht immer ist es ratsam,
mit Freunden berufliche Verpflichtungen einzugehen, doch hier gestaltete sich das Ganze ausgesprochen erfreulich, und Chris Ofili sagt sogar: »Auf gewisse Weise half mir der Prozess der Zusammenarbeit
mit David, zu definieren, wie ich hier leben wollte.« Wichtig für ihn
selbst und für jeden, der hier zu Besuch kommt, war es in Ofilis
Augen, dass Arbeits- und Privatbereich getrennt sind: Daraus ergeben
sich zwei separat definierte, aber miteinander verbundene Räumlich-
keiten. Ein nach Norden ausgerichtetes Atelier mit kleiner Außen-
terrasse ist im rückwärtigen Teil des Erdgeschosses untergebracht; im
Eingangsbereich befindet sich ein Büro, im Keller ein Zeichenstudio.
Darüber liegen vier separate Zimmer.

Clockwise from top left: *From the attic bedroom, the terrace three floors below can be viewed through a cut-out wall section; the shallow terraced building has been extended out on this floor to provide a glazed dining area and terrace; Ofili intends to keep the living space deliberately neutral; a storage wall conceals a toilet cubicle.*

Du haut à gauche, dans le sens des aiguilles d'une montre : *De la chambre située dans le grenier, on peut contempler le petit jardin trois étages plus bas à travers une ouverture dans le mur; à cet étage, l'étroit bâtiment assorti d'un jardinet a été agrandi pour créer un coin*

salle à manger vitré et une terrasse; Ofili tient à garder son espace de séjour délibérément neutre; un placard mural dissimule un W.-C.

Im Uhrzeigersinn von links oben: *Aus dem Schlafzimmer auf dem Dachboden fällt der Blick drei Etagen tiefer durch eine in die Wand geschnittene Öffnung auf die Terrasse; auf dieser Etage wurde das schmale Reihenhaus erweitert, um einem gefliesten Essbereich und einer Terrasse Platz zu bieten; der Wohnbereich soll ganz bewusst neutral wirken, findet der Hausherr; hinter einer Schrankwand versteckt sich eine Toilette.*

London Interiors   Chris Ofili

Clockwise from top left: *The attic bedroom level is accessed via an open-tread, metal and wood staircase; the small light-filled bedroom; the ox-blood-painted stone staircase with its metal handrail is the only original architectural feature remaining in the building; in the bedroom, every conceivable space has been converted to create extra storage.*

Du haut à gauche, dans le sens des aiguilles d'une montre : *On accède à la chambre du grenier par un escalier ouvert en métal et en bois; la petite chambre remplie de lumière; l'escalier en pierre peint couleur sang de bœuf avec sa rampe en métal est le seul vestige de l'architecture originale du bâtiment; dans la chambre, le moindre recoin a été converti en espace de rangement.*

Im Uhrzeigersinn von links oben: *Auf dem Dachboden befindet sich das Schlafzimmer, in das man über eine offene Treppe aus Metall und Holz gelangt; das kleine lichterfüllte Schlafzimmer; nur die ochsenblutrot gestrichene Steintreppe mit Metallgeländer stammt noch aus der Originalausstattung des Hauses; im Schlafzimmer wird selbst der kleinste Winkel als Stauraum genutzt.*

Enfant, Maureen Paley s'habillait tout de noir, vénérait l'artiste Geor-gia O'Keeffe et l'égérie de la mode Diana Vreeland et savait dès l'âge de cinq ans qu'elle vivrait un jour loin de son Amérique natale. Fasci-née par des artistes britanniques tels que Gilbert & George et Francis Bacon, elle s'installa à Londres en 1976, juste à temps pour assister à l'explosion du rock punk. Elle se dit alors que si la musique pouvait désormais être créée sur une simple console à huit pistes dans une chambre à coucher, il n'y avait aucune raison pour que l'art reste confiné dans l'atmosphère formelle d'une galerie. En 1984, sa maison ouvrière victorienne du East End accueillit Interim Art. «C'était plus un théâtre qu'une galerie», explique-t-elle. «A chaque exposition, il fallait refaire tout le décor». Les murs étaient repeints toutes les quatre à six semaines et le seul espace intime était la chambre à cou-cher. Aujourd'hui Interim Art est pratiquement devenu une institution et occupe une ancienne usine désaffectée, toujours dans le East End.

Maureen Paley

As a child, Maureen Paley dressed in black, worshipped artist Geor-gia O'Keeffe and fashion journalist Diana Vreeland, and knew from the age of five that she would eventually live outside her native America. Having become fascinated by British artists such as Gilbert & George and Francis Bacon, she came to London in 1976, perfectly timing her visit to coincide with the punk rock explosion. Reasoning that if music could now be created on an eight-track in a bedroom, there was no reason why art could only be shown in a formal gallery setting. Her East End Victorian terraced house be-came home to Interim Art in 1984. "It was more a theatre than a home," she says; "as each show changed, it was like building a new set." The walls were painted every four to six weeks, and the only personal space was the bedroom. Today Interim Art has moved slightly closer to becoming part of the establishment, occu-pying a converted factory space, still in the East End.

Als Kind kleidete sich Maureen Paley in Schwarz, verehrte die Künst-lerin Georgia O'Keeffe und die Modejournalistin Diana Vreeland. Schon als Fünfjährige wusste sie, dass sie später einmal im Ausland und nicht in ihrer eigentlichen Heimat Amerika leben wollte. 1976 kam sie nach London, magnetisch angezogen von Künstlern wie Gil-bert & George und Francis Bacon. Das Timing war perfekt, war dies doch das Jahr der Punkrock-Explosion, und wenn man mit einem Achtspurgerät im Schlafzimmer Musik aufnehmen kann, was spricht dann dagegen, Kunst auch außerhalb von förmlichen Kunstgalerien zu zeigen? Ihr viktorianisches Reihenhaus im Londoner East End be-herbergte ab 1984 ihre Firma Interim Art. »Es glich eher einem Thea-ter als einem Zuhause«, sagt Maureen Paley. Die Wände wurden alle vier bis sechs Wochen gestrichen, und das Schlafzimmer war der ein-zige wirklich private Raum. Heute hat sich Interim Art dem Kunst-Establishment etwas angenähert und ist in eine umgebaute Fabrik-halle gezogen, allerdings noch im East End.

Below: Paley says she is naturally quite monklike and finds it very cathartic getting rid of things; besides, there is very little storage space anyway. She finds that eliminating the clutter allows you to focus entirely on the art. "People might look at this space and think it's too confining, but if you're at home all day and go out at night, the world becomes your sitting room."

Ci-dessous. Paley, qui a une nature monacale, trouve très libératoire de se débarrasser du superflu. Ce qui tombe bien parce qu'elle manque cruellement d'espaces de rangement. Selon elle, éliminer le fouillis permet de se concentrer entièrement sur l'art. « Les gens qui voient cet endroit le trouveront peut-être trop spartiate, mais quand on travaille à la maison toute la journée et qu'on sort tous les soirs, le monde entier devient votre salon ».

Unten: Sie sei von Natur aus durchaus mönchisch, sagt Paley und empfindet es als kathartisch, sich von Dingen zu befreien. Allerdings verfügt sie auch nur über begrenzten Stauraum. Sich des überflüssigen Krimskrams zu entledigen, ermöglicht einem, sich vollständig auf die Kunst zu konzentrieren, findet Maureen Paley und sagt: »Leute mögen das Gefühl bekommen, dass dieser Raum zu sehr beengen könnte, doch wenn man den ganzen Tag zu Hause verbringt und abends ausgeht, dann wird die Welt zum Wohnzimmer.«

Facing page: White walls, grey-painted floorboards, directional lighting and partitions that double up as display plinths completely disguise the kitchen-office area. Apart from the necessary table and chairs, the only "comfortable" piece of furniture is a black and white 1950s sofa. The yellow Madonna is one of an unlimited edition by Katharina Fritsch.
Above: The kitchen area is as anonymous and functional as the rest of the main living space, with only the presence of a cooker and washing machine distinguishing it from an ordinary office kitchen.

Page de gauche: Des murs blancs, des parquets peints en gris, un éclairage aux spots et des cloisons qui font également office de surfaces d'exposition camouflent entièrement le coin cuisine et bureau. Hormis la table et les chaises, indispensables, le seul meuble « confortable » est un canapé noir et blanc des années 1950. La madone jaune fait partie d'une édition illimitée de Katharina Fritsch.
Ci-dessus: Le coin cuisine est anonyme et fonctionnel comme le reste du séjour principal. Seule la présence de la cuisinière et de la machine à laver la distingue d'une cuisine de bureau ordinaire.

Linke Seite: Weiße Wände, grau gestrichene Fußbodendielen, Richtstrahler und Raumtrenner, die auch als Schaukästen fungieren können, verbergen den Küchen-Büro-Bereich. Neben den notwendigen Stühlen und dem Tisch ist nur noch ein aus den 1950er Jahren stammendes Sofa in Schwarzweiß wirklich »bequem«. Die gelbe Madonna stammt aus einer unlimitierten Auflage von Katharina Fritsch.
Oben: Die Küche ist genauso anonym und funktional eingerichtet wie der übrige Wohnbereich. Nur der Herd und die Waschmaschine unterscheiden sie von einer reinen Büroküche.

Above: The only personal space in the house is the bedroom, which is painted a subtle shade of almond white. Paley admires Gertrude Stein and Colette, who wrote in bed, and does a lot of her paperwork and reading in her Arts and Crafts iron bed.

Right and facing page: Paley probably knows as much about the diversity of the colour white as an Eskimo would. After years of repainting her home every four to six weeks, she has decided that the perfect white is Dulux Super Matt, beating Brilliant White, which she found too dazzling.

Ci-dessus: Le seul endroit personnel de la maison est la chambre, peinte dans un ton subtil blanc dragée. Paley admire Gertrude Stein et Colette qui écrivaient au lit. Elle fait une grande partie de sa paperasse et lit dans son lit en fer Arts and Crafts.

A droite et page de droite: Paley en connaît sûrement autant qu'un Esquimau sur les différentes nuances du blanc. Après avoir repeint sa maison toutes les quatre à six semaines pendant des années, elle a décidé que le blanc le plus parfait était le Dulux Super Matt, qui l'emporte sur le Brilliant White qu'elle juge trop aveuglant.

Oben: Das Schlafzimmer ist der einzig wirklich persönliche Bereich des Hauses. Es ist in einem zarten Mandelweiß gestrichen. Maureen Paley bewundert Gertrude Stein und Colette, die im Bett schrieben, und erledigt selbst auch einen Großteil ihrer Korrespondenz in ihrem Eisenbett im Arts-and-Crafts-Stil. Außerdem liest sie hier.

Rechts und rechte Seite: Wahrscheinlich kennt Maureen Paley die Bandbreite der Farbe Weiß ebenso gut wie die Eskimos. Nachdem sie ihr Zuhause über Jahre hinweg alle vier bis sechs Wochen neu gestrichen hat, steht für sie fest, dass Dulux Supermatt das perfekteste Weiß liefert. Brilliant White leuchtet ihr zu stark.

Dans l'achat d'une propriété, c'est presque toujours cet élément intangible qu'on appelle «la bonne atmosphère» qui nous fait craquer. Lorsque Stephen Palmer et Jacqueline Lucas ont vu pour la première fois cette maison de la fin du 18ᵉ siècle à Hampstead, ils sont immédiatement tombés sous le charme. Toutefois, ils reconnaissent qu'il leur a fallu près de deux ans avant de s'y sentir vraiment chez eux. Mais qu'est-ce que deux ans pour une bâtisse qui évolue depuis trois siècles? Il faut ajouter à cela les modifications apportées par les précédents occupants des lieux, qui avaient un faible pour les meubles anglais surchargés, les rideaux froncés et les montagnes de coussins couleur de mousse, de bruyère et de chocolat. C'était charmant, concèdent les Palmer, mais «pas vraiment notre style». Aujourd'hui, la spacieuse cuisine à plan ouvert et les coins salle à manger et séjour s'accordent étonnamment bien avec les parties anciennes tapissées de lambris en chêne.

Stephen Palmer & Jacqueline Lucas

That intangible thing, "the right atmosphere", is almost always what initially attracts us to a prospective new home. When Stephen Palmer and Jacqueline Lucas originally saw this early Georgian house in Hampstead, they immediately had a good feeling about it, but admit that it's taken almost two years for the place to really feel like home. Two years is a very short time in the context of a house that has been evolving for nearly 300 years. Add to that the contribution made by the previous tenants, who favoured overstuffed English furniture, swagged curtains and piles of cushions in tones of moss, heather and chocolate. "Lovely", the Palmers concede, "but not exactly us", says Jacqueline. Now the large open-plan kitchen, dining and family area extension sits surprisingly comfortably next to the oak panelling of the older part of the house.

Es ist fast immer dieses schwer in Worte zu fassende »gewisse Etwas«, die richtige Atmosphäre, die beim Erwerb eines Hauses den Ausschlag gibt. Als Stephen Palmer und Jacqueline Lucas dieses frühgeorgianische Haus in Hampstead zum ersten Mal sahen, hatten sie sofort ein gutes Gefühl. Allerdings dauerte es noch zwei weitere Jahre, bis sie sich wirklich zu Hause fühlten. Zwei Jahre ist eine kurze Zeit – wenn man bedenkt, dass das Haus schon fast 300 Jahre alt ist und sich immer wieder verändert hat. Dazu kam noch der Geschmack der früheren Bewohner, die eine überladene und vollgestopfte, typisch englische Inneneinrichtung mit wogenden Vorhängen und wahren Kissentürmen in Moosgrün, Heidelila und Schokoladenbraun bevorzugten. »Wunderbar«, sagten die Palmers, »aber nichts für uns.« Heute vertragen sich die große offene Küche, der Ess- und der Wohnbereich erstaunlich gut mit der Eichentäfelung im älteren Teil des Hauses.

Previous page: *The Palmers added bamboo, palms and ornate grasses to the existing weeping willow and ivy in the walled garden.*
Right: *In the family area, the Palmers' daughter Chili – named after John Travolta's character in the film "Get Shorty" – gets to play on a fake mink rug. The fibreglass chaise was designed by Charles and Ray Eames in 1948.*
Below: *The huge American-style fridge is produced by Sub-Zero. Beyond the tropical fish tank, filled with trigger, puffer, bat and angel fish, is a heavily carved table that once belonged to the French actress Sarah Bernhardt.*

Page précédente: *Dans le jardin muré, les Palmer ont rajouté des bambous, des palmiers et des plantes d'ornement pour tenir compagnie au saule pleureur et au lierre.*
A droite: *Dans le coin séjour, Chili, la fille des Palmer qui doit son nom au personnage incarné par John Travolta dans «Get Shorty», peut se rouler à loisir sur le tapis en faux vison. La chaise en fibres de verre a été conçue par Charles et Ray Eames en 1948.*
Ci-dessous: *L'énorme réfrigérateur américain vient de chez Sub-Zero. De l'autre côté de l'aquarium tropical qui abrite des poissons gâchettes, tétrodons, chauve-souris et anges, une lourde table sculptée ayant appartenu autrefois à Sarah Bernhardt.*

Vorhergehende Seite: *Trauerweide und Efeu gab es in dem von einer Mauer umgebenen Garten schon vor den Palmers. Mit ihnen zogen Bambus, Palmen und Ziergras ein.*
Rechts: *In der Familienecke darf Töchterchen Chili – benannt nach John Travoltas Rolle in »Schnappt Shorty« – auf einem Teppich aus falschem Nerz spielen. Den Fiberglasstuhl entwarfen Charles und Ray Eames 1948.*
Unten: *Der riesige amerikanische Kühlschrank stammt von Sub-Zero. Hinter dem Aquarium, in dem sich Drücker- und Fledermausfische sowie Engelhaie tummeln, steht ein reich geschnitzter Tisch, der einst der französischen Schauspielerin Sarah Bernhardt gehörte.*

Above: The Palmers have filled the panelled first-floor drawing room with a collection of modern furniture classics, including Marc Newson's aluminium "Lockheed Lounge", Mies van der Rohe's leather-upholstered daybed and lamps by Tom Dixon and Isamu Noguchi.
Right: the view from the oak-panelled hallway into the drawing room with its silver-painted ceiling. The "Egg" chair is by Arne Jacobsen; in front of it is a "Novage" or cloud light by Guy de Rougemont; and the triangular cushion in the doorway is from the Aman Hotel in Phuket, Thailand.

Ci-dessus: Les Palmer ont rempli le petit salon lambrissé du premier étage avec leur collection de classiques du mobilier contemporain, dont un fauteuil «Lockheed Lounge» en aluminium de Marc Newson, un lit de repos en cuir de Mies van der Rohe et des lampes de Tom Dixon et Isamu Noguchi.
A droite. une vue du petit salon au plafond peint en argent depuis le couloir tapissé de boiseries en chêne. Le fauteuil «Egg» est d'Arne Jacobsen. Devant lui, un «Novage», ou lampe nuage, de Guy de Rougemont. Le coussin triangulaire sur le seuil vient de l'hôtel Aman, à Phuket, en Thaïlande.

Oben: Den mit Paneelen ausgestatteten Salon im ersten Stock haben die Palmers mit modernen Möbeln eingerichtet, darunter Klassiker wie Marc Newsons »Lockheed Lounge« aus Aluminium, Mies van der Rohes lederbezogenes Tagesbett sowie Leuchten von Tom Dixon und Isamu Noguchi.
Rechts: der Blick vom eichengetäfelten Flur in das Wohnzimmer mit seiner in Silber gestrichenen Decke. Den Sessel »Egg« entwarf Arne Jacobsen; davor steht ein »Novage«, ein Wolkenlicht von Guy de Rougemont. Das dreieckige Kisser stammt aus dem Aman-Hotel auf Phuket in Thailand.

Clockwise from top left: Jacqueline's study is dominated by a painted and carved 18th-century Italian wardrobe, in front of which is a "T-chair" by Antonio Citterio and Glen Oliver Löw, bought at Vitra; in the bedroom hangs a "Bubble" chair by Eero Aarnio, while in the background an Alessandro Mendini "Proust's armchair" can be seen; the bathroom; a mobile of Chili's belongings hangs above her bed.

Du haut à gauche, dans le sens des aiguilles d'une montre: Le bureau de Jacqueline est dominé par une armoire italienne du 18e siècle. La chaise «T» d'Antonio Citterio et de Glen Oliver Löw a été achetée chez Vitra; dans la chambre, un fauteuil «Bubble» d'Eero Aarnio. Au fond, le «fauteuil de Proust» d'Alessandro Mendini; la salle de bains; au-dessus du lit de Chili, un mobile réalisé avec ses objets.

Im Uhrzeigersinn von links oben: Das Arbeitszimmer von Jacqueline Lucas beherrscht ein italienischer Schrank aus dem 18. Jahrhundert, der »T«-Stuhl von Antonio Citterio und Glen Oliver Löw wurde bei Vitra erworben; im Schlafzimmer hängt Eero Aarnios »Bubble Chair«, im Hintergrund sieht man Alessandro Mendinis »Proust«-Sessel; das Bad; über Chilis Bett hängt ein Mobile.

London Interiors   Stephen Palmer & Jacqueline Lucas

This huge hearth would have been part of the house's kitchen which is today used by the Palmers as a library. The iron and brass stool is 16th to 17th-century Italian. Jacqueline is sitting on a leather Chesterfield sofa bought at World's End in Chelsea. A 1970s chrome "Sputnik" standing lamp and a coloured-glass "Giocasta" lamp can be seen behind.

A l'origine, l'énorme foyer de cheminée devait faire partie de la cuisine. Aujourd'hui, les Palmer ont converti la pièce en salle de lecture. Le tabouret italien en fer forgé et cuivre date du 16e ou 17e siècle. Jacqueline

est allongée sur un canapé Chesterfield en cuir acheté à World's End à Chelsea. Derrière se tiennent un lampadaire «Spoutnik» en chrome des années 1970 et une lampe «Giocasta» en verre teint.

Diese riesige Feuerstelle gehörte wohl früher zur Küche des Hauses. Heute dient der Raum als Bibliothek. Der Sitz aus Eisen und Messing wurde im 16. oder 17. Jahrhundert in Italien gefertigt. Jacqueline liegt auf einem Chesterfield-Sofa vom World's End in Chelsea. Die »Sputnik«-Stehlampe aus Chrom stammt aus den 1970er Jahren; dahinter sieht man eine »Giocasta«-Leuchte aus gefärbtem Glas.

Souvent imitée, avec plus ou moins de succès, l'architecture de John Pawson a fini par définir le minimalisme contemporain. De fait, combien d'architectes peuvent se targuer d'avoir eu leur nom intégré dans le vocabulaire du design, à l'instar d'un Antoni Gaudí ou d'un Mies van der Rohe? Aujourd'hui, l'adjectif «pawsonien» décrit un espace dépouillé, rempli de lumière et empreint d'une retenue ascétique. C'est un concept qui séduit une partie de chacun d'entre nous, cette partie qui rêve d'une existence dépouillée de tout le «superflu». Mais si cela reste des vœux pieux pour la majorité, John Pawson et sa famille en ont fait leur réalité. Un usage limité des matériaux, en l'occurrence de la Pietra di Lecce, une pierre calcaire italienne aux tons dorés, permet de se concentrer sur la beauté inhérente de la matière brute. Dans le même ordre d'idées, Pawson n'achète que ce dont il a strictement besoin, puis range tout ce dont il ne se sert pas. Il n'y a donc rien d'étonnant à ce qu'on vienne de lui commander la construction d'un monastère de trappistes.

John & Catherine Pawson

Much emulated with varying degrees of success, the architecture of John Pawson has come to define contemporary minimalism. Indeed, how many architects enjoy their name becoming part of the design vernacular, in the way that, say, Antoni Gaudí's or Mies van der Rohe's have? Today, "Pawsonesque" is shorthand for light-filled, empty space and ascetic restraint. His ideas appeal to a part of all of us, the part that dreams of getting rid of all that extraneous "stuff". While this is idle daydreaming for most of us, John Pawson and his family live the reality. Use of a limited range materials, in this case golden Italian Pietra di Lecce limestone, focuses our attention on its inherent beauty. Similarly, Pawson buys only what he needs, and then puts it away when it's not in use. It comes as no surprise, then, that he has recently been commissioned to design a monastery for Trappist monks.

Oft und mit unterschiedlichem Erfolg wurde die Architektur von John Pawson kopiert, die heute den neuen Minimalismus definiert. Dass sein Name jetzt in die Alltagssprache eingegangen ist – wie bei Antoni Gaudí oder Mies van der Rohe –, gelingt nicht vielen Architekten. »Pawsonesque« ist heute ein Synonym für leere, lichterfüllte Räume, die ästhetische Zurückhaltung ausdrücken. Seine Ideen sprechen bis zu einem gewissen Grad zweifellos jeden von uns an – den Teil in uns, der davon träumt, den ganzen überflüssigen Kram einfach loszuwerden. Für die Mehrheit von uns wird dieser Traum wohl ewig ein Tagtraum bleiben; John Pawson und seine Familie leben ihn jedoch. Der Einsatz von einigen wenigen Materialien – in diesem Fall italienischer »Pietra di Lecce«-Kalkstein – ermöglicht die Konzentration auf die dem Rohmaterial innewohnende Schönheit. Aus dem gleichen Grund kauft John Pawson nur Dinge, die er wirklich benötigt, und räumt sie weg, wenn er sie nicht mehr braucht. Und so erstaunt es auch nicht, dass er kürzlich den Auftrag erhalten hat, ein Trappistenkloster zu entwerfen.

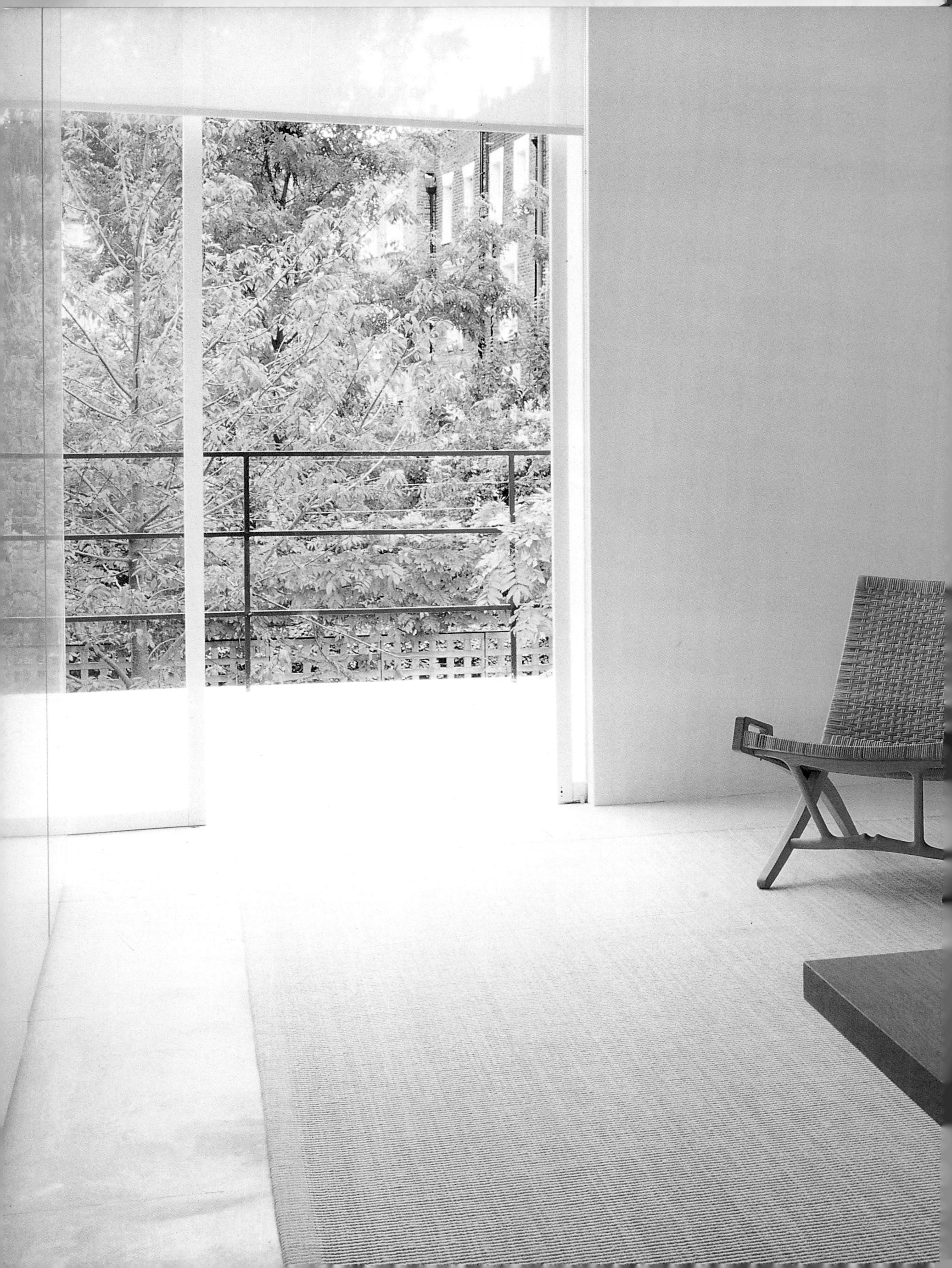

Pour Oliver et Charlie Peyton, les grandes demeures aux façades en stuc blanc et les squares verts au nord de Hyde Park sont le vrai Londres. «C'est un quartier international et anonyme comme dans une vraie ville. Ça n'a rien d'un village de campagne», déclare Peyton en faisant allusion à l'ambiance de Notting Hill qui se trouve à deux pas. Leur appartement, situé au deuxième étage, a une double exposition et domine un des plus beaux squares de la capitale. Son atmosphère très parisienne n'est pas uniquement due aux proportions élégantes de ses pièces ni à ses fenêtres qui vont du sol au plafond. Une grande partie de leurs meubles vient du marché aux puces de Clignancourt. Charlie a été élevée dans des intérieurs classiques, alors qu'Oliver, dont la société Gruppo a révolutionné le monde des bars et des restaurants dans les années 1990, penche plutôt pour le moderne. Ils déclarent à l'unisson que leur appartement est le fruit d'une collaboration «fifty-fifty».

Chelsea n'est pas le genre de quartier où l'on s'attend à trouver un immense loft. L'étage, avec ses quelque 500 cents mètres carrés, est assez vaste pour accueillir l'appartement, les bureaux et les showrooms du décorateur Jonathan Reed, ainsi que la chambre noire de son compagnon, le photographe Ken Hayden. Le bâtiment, qui faisait autrefois partie d'un ensemble de quatre asiles pour indigents construits en 1880 sur King's Road, est le seul qui reste après que les autres furent bombardés. Il a été brièvement annexé par la mairie de Chelsea (Judy Garland s'y est même mariée!), avant d'être converti en hôpital pour femmes, ce qu'il est resté jusque dans les années 1970. Il était abandonné depuis quinze ans quand Reed et Hayden y ont emménagé, il y a deux ans. Reed, aujourd'hui l'un des professionnels les plus recherchés dans le monde très compétitif de la décoration d'intérieur, a transformé cet espace utilitaire avec le style qui a fait sa renommée, entièrement à base de matières et de textures neutres et d'un assortiment impeccable de meubles anciens et modernes.

Jonathan Reed

Chelsea is the unlikely location of this enormous loft-style flat. The whole floor, which measures 5,500 square feet, is large enough to house not just the home, but the offices and showrooms of interior designer Jonathan Reed, as well as the darkroom of his partner, photographer Ken Hayden. Originally one of four, the building was constructed in 1880 on the King's Road as a workhouse, but now stands alone after the others were bombed. Briefly, the premises became an annexe to Chelsea Town Hall – Judy Garland was married there – and then, until the 1970s, it was a women's hospital. Having stood empty for 15 years, Reed and Hayden found dead pigeons everywhere when they moved in a couple of years ago. Reed, who is one of the most sought-after names in the competitive world of interior decorating today, has transformed the utilitarian interior with his signature style of neutral textural materials and impeccable mix of antique and modern furniture.

Diese riesige Wohnung im Loftstil liegt überraschenderweise in Chelsea. Auf der gesamten Etage, die mehr als 500 Quadratmeter misst, befindet sich nicht nur das Zuhause, sondern auch die Büros und Showrooms des Interior Designers Jonathan Reed und die Dunkelkammer seines Partners, des Fotografen Ken Hayden. 1880 wurde das Haus als eines von ursprünglich vier solcher »Workhouses« auf der King's Road errichtet; die anderen fielen dem Bombenhagel zum Opfer. Zwischendurch wurde es für kurze Zeit zum Nebengebäude der Chelsea Town Hall umfunktioniert – hier heiratete sogar Judy Garland – und diente dann bis in die 1970er Jahre als Frauenkrankenhaus. Anschließend war es 15 Jahre lang unbewohnt, und als Reed und Hayden vor einigen Jahren einzogen, entdeckten sie überall tote Tauben. Jonathan Reed gehört zu den begehrtesten Designern in der hart umkämpften Welt der Innenarchitekten und hat das auf Nützlichkeit ausgerichtete Innere des Hauses in seinem typischen Stil eingerichtet: neutrale Materialien und Oberflächen sowie ein makelloser Mix aus antiken und modernen Möbeln.

Above: The 1940s tan leather wing chair is by Danish designer Fritz Henningsen; the pair of 1950s low armchairs are by Paul McCobb. The sisal flooring, which Reed has used throughout the flat, is set into an oak border; the curtains are unlined wool flannel – usually used for suiting – with large metal eyelets hung on nickel poles.
Right: The 1970s leather sofa was found discarded in a friend's garage. The chair and upholstered coffee table standing on the circular Tibetan natural wool rug are by Reed.

Ci-dessus: La bergère en cuir clair, des années 1940, est du créateur danois Fritz Henningsen, et la paire de fauteuils bas des années 1950 de l'Américain Paul McCobb. Dans tout l'appartement, Reed a utilisé un tapis en sisal bordé d'une frise en chêne. Les rideaux sont en flanelle non bordée, du type qu'on utilise pour les costumes, avec de gros œillets métalliques glissant sur des tringles en nickel.
A droite: Le canapé en cuir des années 1970 a été découvert dans le garage d'un ami. Le fauteuil et la table basse tapissés, posés sur un tapis circulaire tibétain en laine naturelle, sont de Reed.

Oben: Der dänische Designer Fritz Henningsen entwarf diesen Ohrensessel aus hellem Leder in den 1940er Jahren. Das niedrige Sesselpaar aus den 1950er Jahren hingegen stammt von Paul McCobb. Jonathan Reed hat die ganze Wohnung mit Sisalteppich auslegen und mit Bodenleisten aus Eiche versehen lassen. Der Vorhangstoff besteht aus ungefüttertem Wollflanell, der eigentlich für Herrenanzüge verwendet wird. Die Vorhänge hängen mit Hilfe großer Metallösen an vernickelten Vorhangstangen.
Rechts: Das Ledersofa aus den 1970er Jahren wurde in der Garage eines Freundes entdeckt. Der Sessel und der bezogene Couchtisch sind Entwürfe von Jonathan Reed. Sie stehen auf einem kreisrunden tibetanischen Teppich aus naturbelassener Wolle.

London Interiors   Jonathan Reed

Right: A 1920s French pearwood and mahogany woven cabinet stands in front of the central partition. The chairs on either side are by Jules-Emile Leleu and the nickel-plated wall sconces above are by Reed. Reed also designed the bleached oak oval table with bronze feet, on which stands a 1960s Dutch circular sculpture in black marble.

Below: The bedroom area is a continuation of the main space. On the Burmese teak colonial bed is a blanket woven from undyed camel hair. Two "Best-lites" are wall-mounted above a pair of American military-issue chests from the 1940s.

A droite: Une armoire française des années 1920, en tressage de lames de poirier et d'acajou. Elle est encadrée par des chaises de Leleu et d'une paire d'appliques plaquées de nickel de Reed. Ce dernier a également conçu la table ovale en chêne décoloré aux pieds en bronze. Dessus, une sculpture circulaire hollandaise en marbre noir des années 1960.

Ci-dessous: Le coin chambre à coucher est un prolongement du vaste espace de séjour. Sur le lit colonial birman en teck, une couverture tissée en poils de chameau non teintés. Deux «Best-lites» sont accrochées au mur en guise de lampes de chevet, au-dessus d'une paire de coffres militaires américains des années 1940.

Rechts: Aus Birnenholz- und Mahagonistreifen ist dieser französische Schrank aus den 1920er Jahren geflochten. Die zwei Stühle sind von Jules-Emile Leleu. Die vernickelten Wandleuchter hat der Hausherr entworfen, ebenso der ovalen Tisch aus gebleichter Eiche mit Bronzefüßen. Darauf steht eine runde Skulptur aus schwarzem Marmor, die in den 1960er Jahren in Holland gefertigt wurde.

Unten: Der Schlafbereich befindet sich am Rand des Wohnbereichs. Auf dem burmesischen Teakholzbett im Kolonialstil liegt eine Decke aus ungefärbtem Kamelhaar. Über den beiden Kommoden, die aus dem Bestand der amerikanischen Armee aus den 1940er Jahren stammen, hängen zwei Lampen, so genannte »Best-lites«.

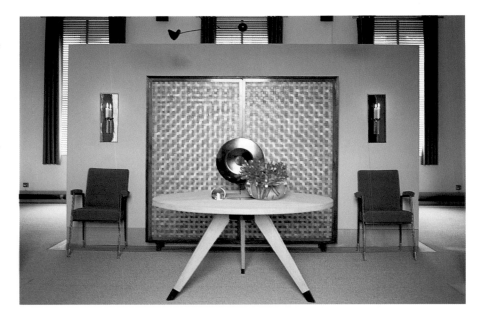

Below: The bathroom was originally the scrubbing-up room for the hospital and it's here that the flat's utilitarian origins are most apparent. While the large windows throughout provide lots of lovely light, they posed a particular problem in the planning of this area. Reed resolved this by placing the shower in the corner and by building two low walls on either side. Natural teak was used for a slatted shelf below the ceramic butler's sink, for the shower floor and for the bath surround. The floor is covered in rubber and the radiator is nickel-plated. Standard-issue tiles were used on the walls and the venetian blinds are aluminium.

Ci-dessous: C'est dans la salle de bains, ancienne salle d'eau de l'hôpital, que l'on sent le plus le passé utilitaire des lieux. Si les hautes fenêtres assurent une belle lumière, elles n'ont pas été sans poser de problèmes que Reed a résolus en plaçant la douche dans l'angle et en érigeant deux murets de chaque côté. L'étagère sous l'évier d'office en céramique, le sol de la douche et le pourtour de la baignoire sont en lattes de teck naturel. Le sol est recouvert d'un tapis en caoutchouc Dalsouple et le radiateur est plaqué de nickel. Les murs sont tapissés de carrelage réglementaire et les stores vénitiens sont en aluminium.

Unten: Das heutige Badezimmer diente ursprünglich als Waschraum des Krankenhauses. Hier ist der auf Nützlichkeit ausgerichtete Charakter der Wohnung am deutlichsten sichtbar. Während die großen Fenster überall sonst für schönes Licht sorgten, stellten sie im Bad ein Problem dar. Jonathan Reed löste es, in dem er die Dusche in der Ecke unterbrachte und zu beiden Seiten zwei niedrige Mauern einzog. Für die Platte unter dem Waschbecken, einem »Butler's Sink«, wurde ebenso wie für den Duschboden und die Badewanneneinfassung naturbelassenes Teakholz verwendet. Der Boden ist mit Kautschuk ausgelegt, der Heizkörper wurde vernickelt, an den Wänden handelsübliche Fliesen und Jalousien aus Aluminium.

Facing page: Since the apartment is completely open-plan, with only one partition separating the sleeping area from the main living area, the kitchen has been designed to be as unobtrusive as possible. The metal hanging lights originally came from Manchester Library and date from the 1920s: on the ceiling the original ventilation channels are still in place.
Above: Above the tile and slate fireplace is a patinated wood sculpture by Graham Day. The iconic, mandala-like image is in fact a commonly seen London drain cover that has been enlarged to such an extent that its prosaic origins are obscured.

Page de gauche: L'appartement étant composé d'un grand espace avec une seule cloison pour isoler la chambre, la cuisine a été conçue la plus discrète possible. Les plafonniers en métal viennent de la bibliothèque municipale de Manchester et datent des années 1920, tandis que les conduits d'aération dans le plafond sont restés en place.
Ci-dessus: au-dessus de la cheminée en carrelage et ardoise, une sculpture en bois patiné de Graham Day. Le motif iconographique qui rappelle un mandala n'est en fait qu'une reproduction d'un vulgaire couvercle de bouche d'égout londonien, agrandi au point qu'on le ne reconnaît plus.

Linke Seite: Das gesamte Apartment ist offen konzipiert, nur zwischen Schlaf- und Wohnbereich gibt es eine Trennwand. Die Küche wurde bewusst unauffällig gestaltet. Die Hängelampen aus Metall stammen aus einer Bücherei in Manchester und wurden in den 1920er Jahren gefertigt. An der Decke sind noch die ursprünglichen Belüftungsschlitze sichtbar.
Oben: Auf dem gekachelten Kaminsims mit Schiefereinfassung steht eine patinierte Holzskulptur von Graham Day. Sie erinnert an eine Ikone oder ein Mandala, ist aber in Wirklichkeit den Kanaldeckeln entlehnt, wie man sie in London überall sieht. Durch die Vergrößerung ist der prosaische Ursprung nicht mehr erkennbar.

Portobello Road, London W11

Sarah Kean et Sam Robinson, dont la bijouterie The Cross a pris une ampleur planétaire depuis le lancement de leur catalogue sur Internet, ne sont pas encore revenues de l'extraordinaire impact qu'elles ont eu sur la vente au détail. Meilleures amies du monde depuis l'âge de 17 ans, elles ont conçu le projet de leur boutique dans le studio de Robinson à Notting Hill. Sans cet appartement à la grandeur fanée, il n'y aurait sans doute jamais eu de phénomène «The Cross». La pièce aux belles proportions, avec son haut plafond et ses pâtisseries, est un cahier d'esquisses en trois dimensions, le lieu où elles testent leurs idées et expérimentent de nouveaux produits. La maison de Robinson, comme la boutique, regorge d'un exubérant mélange de babioles en grillage, de chic bohème et de style désuet anglais. Leur philosophie d'achat est simple: se fier à son instinct. Si un objet est beau dans l'appartement, il le sera également dans la boutique. «Certaines choses sont ici parce qu'elles sont belles», déclare Robinson, «d'autres simplement parce qu'elles nous font rire».

Sam Robinson

Sarah Kean and Sam Robinson, whose bijou emporium The Cross has now gone global with the launch of their online catalogue site, are bemused by the extraordinary impact they have had on retailing. Best mates since they were 17, they hatched the plan for the shop in Robinson's fadingly grand Notting Hill studio flat and it's fair to say that without the flat there would probably be no Cross phenomenon. The beautifully proportioned room, with its high ceilings and ornate plasterwork, is their three-dimensional scrapbook. Robinson's home, like the shop, is crammed with an exuberant mix 'n' match collection of girlie trinkets, bohemian chic and shabby English style. Their buying philosophy is simple: they just go with their gut feeling. If it looks good in the flat, it goes in the shop too. "We have some things because they are beautiful," says Robinson, "but others just because they make us laugh."

Sarah Kean und Sam Robinson, deren Laden The Cross dank einer Website mittlerweile weltweit präsent ist, sind über den außergewöhnlichen Einfluss, den sie auf den Einzelhandel haben, etwas verwundert. Schon mit 17 Jahren waren sie die dicksten Freundinnen. Zusammen heckten sie in Sam Robinsons winziger Wohnung in Notting Hill – mehr verblichene als tatsächliche Pracht – auch den Plan für ihren gemeinsamen Laden aus. Man darf wohl behaupten, dass es ohne diese Wohnung auch kein »The Cross«-Phänomen gäbe. Der wunderschön proportionierte Raum mit hohen Decken und aufwendigem Stuck ist ihr dreidimensionaler Scribble-Block. Hier entwickeln sie ihre Ideen und experimentieren mit neuen Produkten. Wie ihr Geschäft ist auch Sam Robinsons Wohnung vollgestopft mit einem übersprudelnden Mix aus Boheme-Chic und klassisch-englischem, wenn auch etwas abgewetztem Stil. Ihre Kaufphilosophie ist einfach – sie hören auf ihren Instinkt und wissen, dass Dinge, die in der Wohnung gut aussehen, auch im Geschäft wirken werden. »Einiges besitzen wir, weil es schön ist«, erklärt Sam Robinson. »Anderes einfach nur, weil es uns zum Lachen bringt.«

Previous page: Believe it or not this is Robinson's work desk.
Above: Every corner of the flat is a riot of silky embroidered fabrics and frocks, jewel-coloured cushions, and decaying paint and gilt, while the surfaces are covered in a magpie collection of girlie accessories and kitsch. Inexplicably, this eclectic approach to decorating also manages to disguise the lack of space.
Right: A kitchenette and bed-platform share one section of the room, and below the bed is the bathroom and entrance doorway.

Page précédente: Voici le bureau sur lequel Robinson travaille!
Ci-dessus: Chaque recoin de l'appartement est un patchwork d'étoffes soyeuses brodées, de fripes, de coussins chatoyants, de peinture écaillée et de dorures. La moindre surface croule sous des piles d'accessoires féminins et d'objets kitsch. Etrangement, cette décoration éclectique fait paraître l'appartement plus grand qu'il ne l'est réellement.
A droite: Une partie de la pièce est occupée par une kitchenette et un lit en mezzanine. Sous le lit, la salle de bains et la porte d'entrée.

Vorhergehende Seite: Ob man es glaubt oder nicht, so sieht Sam Robinsons Arbeitsplatz aus!
Oben: Jeder Winkel der Wohnung quillt über vor bestickten Seidenstoffen, Kleidern, Kissen in den Farben von Edelsteinen, abblätternder Farbe und verblichener Goldauflage – und sämtliche verfügbaren Oberflächen sind zudem mit einer frechen Sammlung von Girlie-Accessoires und Kitsch bedeckt. Völlig unerklärlich ist, dass dieser außergewöhnliche Deko-Touch den Mangel an Platz überspielt.
Rechts: Eine kleine Küche und ein Hochbett teilen sich einen Bereich des Raums. Unter dem Hochbett befinden sich Badezimmer und Eingangsflur.

London Interiors   Sam Robinson

Robinson and Lilly, her Staffordshire bull terrier. Robinson has lived in the studio flat for seven years, but has been a Notting Hill girl for more than twelve. Her instinctive "Notting Hill girlie bo-ho chic" style is what has made The Cross such a success.

Robinson et Lilly, son Staffordshire bull-terrier. Robinson a emménagé dans ce studio il y a sept ans mais habite le quartier depuis douze. Son sens inné du «baba cool chic à la Notting Hill» est en grande partie à l'origine du succès de The Cross.

Sam Robinson und ihr Staffordshire Bullterrier Lilly. Seit sieben Jahren bewohnt Sam Robinson diese kleine Wohnung; seit 12 Jahren allerdings gehört sie schon zur Notting-Hill-Clique. Ihr »Notting Hill girlie bo-ho chic« war es, der The Cross zu seinem großen Erfolg verholfen hat.

London Interiors Sam Robinson

Clockwise from top left: *the tiny sink area in the kitchenette; Polaroids, postcards and a pink acrylic vase by Le Page fight for attention on the marble mantelpiece; an encrustation of shells and starfish disguises the rather ordinary bathroom; Robinson has a passion for flowers – silk ones in her hair, plastic in the bathroom and real ones in the kitchen.*

Du haut à gauche, dans le sens des aiguilles d'une montre: *le minuscule coin évier de la kitchenette; des Polaroïds, des cartes postales et un vase rose en acrylique de Le Page se disputent la première place*

sur le manteau de cheminée en marbre; une frise de coquillages et d'étoiles de mer incrustés donne de la personnalité à une salle de bains sans signes particuliers; Robinson a une passion pour les fleurs.

Im Uhrzeigersinn von links oben: *das winzige Spülbecken in der Küchenzeile; auf dem marmornen Kaminsims buhlen Polaroidfotos, Postkarten una eine pinkfarbene Acrylvase von Le Page um Aufmerksamkeit; das eher banale Badezimmer wird durch den Seestern- und Muschelbewuchs etwas Besonderes; Sam Robinsons Leidenschaft sind Blumen aller Art.*

On ne s'attend guère à voir un designer spécialisé dans les meubles élémentaires, géométriques et conceptuels habitant dans une villa à tourelles du début du siècle dans le quartier verdoyant de Fulham. C'est pourtant là que Rolf Sachs s'est établi depuis cinq ans. Il a choisi cet endroit principalement pour l'espace, la hauteur sous plafond et la lumière naturelle qui lui permettent d'exposer au mieux son extraordinaire collection de sièges. Si les chaises mémorables sont rares, certaines sont capables d'exprimer de manière éclatante les comportements, les idées et les valeurs d'une société, au point de revêtir un statut iconographique. Sachs applique des règles strictes de pureté et d'objectivité mais sa collection va des œuvres décoratives et ouvragées de Bugatti aux créations les plus récentes, en passant par des chaises en fibres de verre d'Eames. La combinaison de disciplines esthétiques aussi diverses est étonnamment harmonieuse, confirmant l'idée qu'un bon design peut se fondre dans n'importe quel environnement, même dans un quartier aux allures si vieillottes que Fulham.

Rolf Sachs

An Edwardian turreted villa in leafy Fulham is an unlikely address for a designer who specialises in elemental, geometric, conceptual furniture. But it is here that Rolf Sachs has installed his trilingual family for the past five years. He chose the house primarily because it provides the space, high ceilings and copious amounts of natural light needed to display his extraordinary collection of chairs. While memorable chair design is rare, it sometimes vividly expressing the attitudes, ideas and values of a society, eventually taking on iconic status. Sachs' rigid requirement of his own work is that it should be pure and objective, but his collection ranges from the fine decorative work of Carlo Bugatti through Eames' fibreglass to the present day. The combination of such diverse aesthetic disciplines is surprisingly harmonious, supporting the notion that if a piece of design is good, it will work in any environment – even conservative Fulham.

Eine edwardianische Villa mit Türmchen im grünen Stadtteil Fulham ist eine ungewöhnliche Adresse für einen Designer, dessen Möbelentwürfe elementar, geometrisch und konzeptuell sind. Doch hier hat Rolf Sachs seit fünf Jahren seine dreisprachige Familie untergebracht. Bei der Wahl des Hauses war vor allem ausschlaggebend, dass es über den Platz, die hohen Räume und viel natürliches Licht verfügte, um seiner Sammlung außergewöhnlicher Stühle den richtigen Rahmen zu geben. Wirklich gutes, unverwechselbares Stuhl-Design ist selten. Nur manchmal gelingt es, einem Stuhl die Ansichten, Meinungen, Ideen und Werte einer ganzen Gesellschaft zu verleihen und ihn damit zu einer Art Ikone zu machen. Rolf Sachs stellt an sich selbst die strikte Anforderung, rein und objektiv zu arbeiten. Seine Sammlung hingegen spiegelt eine Bandbreite wider – vom feinen, dekorativen Ansatz eines Carlo Bugatti über die Fiberglasentwürfe des Ehepaares Eames bis zum heutigen Design. Die Kombination solcher unterschiedlicher ästhetischer Disziplinen zeigt ein überraschend harmonisches Ergebnis und beweist, dass gutes Design in jedem Umfeld funktioniert – selbst im konservativen Fulham.

First page: *In the ante-room to the main living room, Sachs designed these lead-wrapped MDF boxes to be multifunctional.*
Above: *Looking in the other direction, a "Ping-Pong table" by Ron Arad and a painting by Walter Dahn above the fireplace.*

Première page: *Dans l'antichambre du salon principal, Sachs a conçu les casiers tapissés de plomb de sorte à ce qu'ils puissent remplir de nombreuses fonctions.*
Ci-dessus: *dans la même pièce vue d'un autre angle, une «table de ping-pong» de Ron Arad. Au-dessus de la cheminée, un tableau de Walter Dahn.*

Eingangsseite: *Für den Vorraum zum großen Wohnzimmer entwarf Rolf Sachs diese mit Blei ummantelten, multifunktionalen MDF-Holz-Kisten.*
Oben: *Blickt man in die andere Richtung, entdeckt man Ron Arads »Ping-Pong«-Tisch und über dem Kamin ein Bild von Walter Dahn.*

Clockwise from top left: *in the bedroom, a huge Polaroid by Verner Pawlok, a chair by André Dubreuil, and Sachs' felt roll called "E geil"; the bar, above a portrait by Thomas Ruff; Ron Arad's metal chair and Sachs' chair (1995); the Louis Quinze desk is flanked by Tom Dixon's "Kitchen" chair (1987) and Sachs' two-piece chair.*

Du haut à gauche, dans le sens des aiguilles d'une montre: *dans la chambre à coucher, un Polaroïd géant de Verner Pawlok, une chaise d'André Dubreuil et un rouleau de feutre de Sachs baptisé «E geil»; au-dessus du bar est accroché un portrait par Thomas Ruff; un fau-teuil en métal de Ron Arad et une chauffeuse de Sachs, de 1995; le bu-reau Louis Quinze est flanqué d'une chaise «Kitchen» de Tom Dixon (1987) et d'une chaise en deux morceaux de Sachs.*

Im Uhrzeigersinn von links oben: *Im Schlafzimmer finden sich ein riesiges Polaroidfoto von Verner Pawlok, ein Stuhl von André Dubreuil und Rolf Sachs' Filzrolle, genannt »E geil«; über der Bar hängt ein Porträt von Thomas Ruff; Ron Arads Metallsessel und Sachs' eigener Stuhl (1995); der Louis-Quinze-Schreibtisch ist flankiert von Tom Dixons »Kitchen« (1987) und Sachs' zweiteiligem Stuhl.*

Previous pages: Sachs' collection of chairs, including Frank Gehry's
cardboard "Little Beaver" (1980), and, flanking the fireplace, a pair of
rare Bugatti "Cobra" chairs (1902).
Left: Around the living-room table are two Ron Arad slatted
"Schizzo" chairs (1989) and a woven-rush Tom Dixon "S" chair
(1988). To the left is Sachs' "Chip on the Shoulder" chair.
Above: Covering the bed is a Japanese quilt and above it a photograph by Annelies Strba.

Double page précédente: La collection de sièges de Sachs, dont un
fauteuil en carton de Frank Gehry, «Little Beaver» (1980). et une
paire de chaises de Bugatti, «Cobra» (1902), pièces rares.
A gauche: La table du salon est entourée de deux chaises en lames de
Ron Arad, «Schizzo» (1989) et d'une chaise «S» en jonc tressé de
Tom Dixon (1988). Sur la gauche, on aperçoit une chaise de Sachs,
«Chip on the Shoulder».
Ci-dessus: sur le lit, une couette japonaise. Au-dessus, une photogra-
phie d'Annelies Strba.

Vorhergehende Doppelseite: Rolf Sachs' Stuhlsammlung: beispielsweise Frank Gehrys »Little Beaver« aus Wellpappe (1980) und ein
Paar von Bugattis seltenen »Cobra«-Stühlen aus dem Jahr 1902.
Links: Um den Esstisch stehen Ron Arads Lattenstühle »Schizzo«
(1989), ein »S«-Sessel aus Binsengeflecht von Tom Dixon und links
der Rolf-Sachs-Entwurf »Chip on the Shoulder«.
Oben: Als Bettdecke dient ein japanischer Quilt. Die Fotografie über
dem Bett stammt von Annelies Strba.

*Ces dernières années ont été plutôt déroutantes pour l'homme mo-
derne. Confronté au barrage du politiquement correct et à un monde
en mutation qui semble privilégier les qualités féminines dans presque
tous les domaines, notamment au travail, à quels saints un célibataire
endurci doit-il se vouer? Peter Saville semble avoir résolu ce dilemme
chez lui en se créant une garçonnière résolument provocante avec
l'aide de son codirecteur artistique Mike Meire et du décorateur Ben
Kelly. «J'adore quand on entre dans l'immeuble, qu'on prend l'ascenseur jusqu'au quatrième étage et qu'on pénètre tout à coup dans un
autre monde. Tout est parfaitement orchestré», déclare Mike Meire de
cet immeuble d'appartements construit dans les années 1970 dans le
quartier guindé de Mayfair. La décoration s'inspire de cette décennie,
remise au goût des années 1990. L'effet est moins kitsch, plus soigné.
La démarche est ironique, délibérée et directe. Si le décor pouvait par-
ler, il lancerait sur un ton de défi: «Je suis ce que je suis. Ça vous dé-
range, et alors?». Une vraie bouffée d'air frais!*

Peter Saville

It has been a very confusing time for the modern man in recent
years. Faced by a barrage of political correctness and a changing
world that seems to favour feminine qualities over male in almost
all arenas, especially at work, what is a bona fide bachelor to do?
Peter Saville seems to have solved this conundrum at home by de-
signing this gloriously defiant shag-pad of a penthouse in collaboration with fellow art director Mike Meire and designer Ben Kelly.
"I love it when you walk into the building, take the lift to the fourth
floor, and step into this other world; it's so orchestrated," says
Mike Meire of the 1970s-built flat in conservative Mayfair. Key elements have been taken from that decade and given a 1990s update.
The look is slicker, less tacky and its stance is ironic, knowing and
unapologetic. If this interior could speak, it would be saying defi-
antly: "Look, I know what I am, so sue me." How refreshing.

*Sehr verwirrend waren die vergangenen Jahre für den modernen
Mann. Er sah sich konfrontiert mit den Direktiven der »political correctness« und den Ansprüchen einer sich ändernden Welt, die fast
überall weibliche Eigenschaften den männlichen vorzuziehen scheint,
besonders am Arbeitsplatz. Was bleibt einem eingefleischten Junggesellen da noch? Für sein Zuhause zumindest scheint Peter Saville dieses Rätsel gelöst zu haben. Mit Hilfe des Art-Director-Kollegen Mike
Meire und des Designers Ben Kelly wurde aus seinem Penthouse eine
nur dem Vergnügen dienende Lotterbude. Für Eingeweihte: ein »shag
pad«. »Ich finde es wundervoll, dieses Gebäude zu betreten, den
Fahrstuhl zum 4. Stock zu nehmen und plötzlich in einer anderen
Welt zu sein«, sagt Mike Meire über die in den 1970er Jahren gebaute
Wohnung im konservativen Stadtteil Mayfair. Schlüsselelemente aus
diesem Jahrzehnt wurden aufgegriffen und mit einer 1990er-Jahre-Kur
aufgefrischt. Der Look ist lässiger, weniger geschmacklos, der Blick-
winkel ist ironisch – wissend und unverfroren. Wenn dieses Interieur
sprechen könnte, dann würde es mit Nachdruck erklären: »Hört zu,
ich weiß, was ich bin: na und? Verklagt mich doch!« Wie erfrischend!*

Previous page: *The bedroom can only be saying one thing loud and clear: in the words of spoof 1960s private agent Austin Powers, it's completely "Shagadellic!"*
Below: *Kelly says their approach was to treat the space as a minimalist colour field, adding just a few key elements that played off the existing interior. In a carefree bachelor's kitchen, arguably the most useful key element would have to be his very own Stepford wifelet.*

Page précédente: *La chambre ne cache pas son jeu, elle le crie haut et fort. Pour reprendre les termes d'Austin Powers, l'agent secret déjanté des années 1960, elle est complètement «sexédélique!».*
Ci-dessous: *D'après Kelly, l'espace a été traité comme un champ de couleurs minimaliste. On n'y a ajouté que quelques éléments clefs pour renforcer et contraster avec le décor existant. Dans cette cuisine de célibataire impénitent, il ne manquait plus qu'une épouse modèle aux fourneaux.*

Vorhergehende Seite: *Das Schlafzimmer sagt laut und deutlich, wofür es gedacht ist ... es ist »shagadellic«, wie es der neue Kultstar und nicht ganz Bond-reife Agent Austin Powers beschreiben würde.*
Unten: *Ben Kelly beschreibt seinen Ansatz so: Sie hätten den Raum als minimalistisches Farbfeld gesehen und nur hier und da einige Elemente hinzugefügt, die mit dem bereits existierenden Interieur wetteifern. So muss das Schlüsselelement der unbeschwerten Küche, wie es sich für einen Junggesellen gehört, wohl die hauseigene Hausfrau aus Stepford sein.*

Above: Built in the mid-1970s, the flat was already fitted out with smoked glass and tinted mirrors.
Right: Luxury underfoot has got to be wall-to-wall carpet and a huge sheepskin rug. This, together with the black lacquer coffee table and abundant white scented lilies, all create a comfortable Playboy-playpen of a living room.
Following doublepage: "This is a hard-edged, penthouse dream of a home," says Saville. Charles and Ray Eames designed the "Soft Pad" swivel and tilting chair, while the pink padded satin artwork by Stephen Hepworth is titled "Simply the Best".

Ci-dessous: Datant du milieu des années 1970, l'appartement était déjà équipé de vitres fumées et de miroirs teintés.
A droite: On foule aux pieds le luxe sur l'épaisse moquette et l'immense tapis. Une table basse en laque noire et une abondance de lys blancs parfumés ajoutent à l'atmosphère de lupanar à la «Playboy».
Double page suivante: «C'est vraiment une garçonnière de rêve», confie Saville. Le fauteuil a été dessiné par Charles et Ray Eames, tandis que le tableau en satin rose rembourré, intitulé «Simply the best» est signé Stephen Hepworth.

Oben: Die Wohnung wurde Mitte der 1970er Jahre gebaut und verfügte damals schon über Rauchglas und getönte Spiegel.
Rechts: Fußsohlen-Luxus – das ist der im gesamten Raum verlegte Teppich. Ein schwarzer Lackcouchtisch und intensiv duftende weiße Lilien im Überfluss verstärken den Eindruck einer Spielzeughöhle für kleine Playboy-Tiger.
Folgende Doppelseite: Es sei »ein Penthouse-Traumhaus, allerdings mit Ecken und Kanten«, sagt Peter Saville. Die aus pinkfarbenem gepolstertem Satin gearbeitete Wandskulptur stammt von Stephen Hepworth und heißt schlicht »Simply the Best«.

Fournier Street, London E1

Si l'on se prend parfois à rêver d'une existence plus simple, peu d'entre nous s'imaginent vivant en permanence sans le confort moderne. Ann Shore, directrice artistique et styliste, est persuadée qu'il existe une tendance réelle vers un mode de vie plus naturel et vit ses convictions jusqu'au bout dans cette maison bringuebalante du 18ᵉ siècle à Spital-fields. Le réfrigérateur, le téléphone, le répondeur et une machine à écrire anachronique sont ses seules concessions à la modernité. L'eau chaude est fournie par un Aga des années 1930 alimenté au charbon. Il y a des cheminées dans toutes les pièces et on s'y éclaire de préfé-rence à la bougie. Shore dirige son entreprise innovatrice de vente au détail depuis chez elle, proposant des vêtements et des objets de collec-tion rapportés de ses voyages. A l'origine, Spitalfields était un prospère centre de tissage de la soie mais, lorsque ce secteur déclina, les ouvriers emportèrent leurs métiers à tisser chez eux et transformèrent les der-niers étages de leurs maisons en ateliers, devenant des précurseurs du travail à domicile, version 1800.

Ann Shore

While we all occasionally fantasize about a simple life, few of us could imagine living without our modern conveniences perma-nently. Creative director and stylist Ann Shore believes there is a real trend towards a more low-key as opposed to a high-tech lifestyle and has the courage to live out her convictions in this higg-ledy-piggledy early Georgian Spitalfields house. The fridge, tele-phone, answering machine and a vintage word processor are the only mod cons she allows herself. Hot water is provided by a 1930s coal-fuelled Aga, fireplaces heat every room and candles are pre-ferred to electric lighting. Shore also runs her innovative retail busi-ness from home, selling clothing and collectables picked up on her travels. Originally Spitalfields was a thriving Huguenot silk-weaving centre, but when the industry went into decline, the looms were brought home and the top floors converted into weaving studios – the original live and work concept, 1800s style.

Sicher träumt jeder manchmal vom einfachen Leben, aber nur die wenigsten können sich vorstellen, für immer auf die Bequemlichkeiten der Moderne zu verzichten. Ann Shore, Kreativdirektorin und Styli-stin, glaubt fest daran, dass sich gerade ein neuer Trend weg vom Hightech-Lifestyle und hin zum einfacheren Leben entwickelt. Und sie hat den Mut, ihre Überzeugungen auszuleben: in diesem frühgeor-gianischen Haus in Spitalfields. Kühlschrank, Telefon, Anrufbeantwor-ter und ein veralteter Computer sind die einzigen Zugeständnisse an die Errungenschaften des modernen Lebens, die sie sich erlaubt. Ein Kohleherd aus den 1930er Jahren liefert heißes Wasser, jeder Raum wird per Kamin beheizt und Kerzen ersetzen das elektrische Licht. Von hier betreibt Ann Shore auch ihr innovatives Geschäft und ver-kauft Kleidung und Sammlerstücke, die sie von ihren Reisen mit-bringt. Früher florierte die Seidenweberei im Stadtteil Spitalfields mit seiner hugenottischen Bevölkerung. Nach dem Niedergang der Indu-strie brachte man die Webstühle nach hause und baute die Oberge-schosse der Häuser zu Webzimmern um – der Ursprung des »live and work concept« anno 1800.

Previous pages: *A small terrace overlooks the neighbouring rooftops, chimneystacks and the spire of the famous 18th-century Christ Church by Nicholas Hawksmoor. Box and laurel are planted in Provençal terracotta pots sitting next to rush baskets from Cyprus on the pine decking.*
Right: *Below a piece of Egyptian decorative ironwork stand two French 19th-century "skeps" of willow, cow dung and lime construction, originally used for catching swarms of wild bees.*
Below: *A view from the living room reveals the "garden room".*

Double page précédente: *Une petite terrasse donne sur les toits, les cheminées et le clocher de la célèbre église Christ Church, construite au 18e siècle par Nicholas Hawksmoor. Sur le plancher en sapin, du buis et du laurier plantés dans des pots provençaux en terre cuite sont posés près de paniers chypriotes en jonc tressé.*
A droite: *Sous un élément décoratif égyptien en fer forgé, deux ruches françaises du 19e siècle, en saule, bouse de vache et chaux, conçues à l'origine pour piéger les essaims d'abeilles sauvages.*
Ci-dessous: *Du séjour, on aperçoit le salon-jardin.*

Vorhergehende Doppelseite: *Von der kleinen Terrasse blickt man über die Dächer, Schornsteine und den berühmten Turm der Christ Church von Nicholas Hawksmoor aus dem 18. Jahrhundert. Auf den Planken aus Pinienholz stehen Buchsbaum und Lorbeer in provenzalischen Terrakottatöpfen neben Weidenkörben aus Zypern.*
Rechts: *Unter einem Eisenornament aus Ägypten befinden sich zwei Bienenkörbe, die ursprünglich zum Einfangen wilder Bienen verwendet wurden. Sie stammen aus dem Frankreich des 19. Jahrhunderts und bestehen aus Weidengeflecht, Kuhdung und Kalk.*
Unten: *Ein Blick aus dem Wohnzimmer auf den »garden room«.*

Above: The living room is a masculine-feminine mix of rough materials: wood, stone and leather, with soft decorative elements such as the pure linen slip covers on the armchairs and the 19th-century velvet and gilt brocade, ottoman cushions in front of the wood fire.
Right: Hanging against painted wood panelling is a selection of Shore's antique Indian saris and woven bags from Africa and Bali. On the floor is a 19th-century flock-carpet-covered Moroccan chest, Afghan textiles and a pair of Moroccan slippers.

Ci-dessus: Le salon est décoré d'un assortiment masculin-féminin, les matières brutes – bois, pierre et cuir – étant tempérées par des touches décoratives plus suaves telles que les housses en lin pur sur les fauteuils et les coussins ottomans du 19ᵉ siècle en brocart de velours et d'or posés devant la cheminée.
A droite: accroché aux lambris en bois peint, un échantillon de la collection de Shore de saris anciens et de sacs tissés africains et balinais. Sur le sol, un coffre marocain du 19ᵉ siècle recouvert d'un tapis en bourre de laine, des étoffes afghanes et une paire de babouches marocaines.

Oben: Im Wohnzimmer mischen sich maskuline und feminine Elemente. Grobes Holz, Stein und Leder sind mit weichen Oberflächen dekoriert, wie den reinleinenen Sesselbezügen und den Hockerkissen aus Samt und Goldbrokat, die vor dem holzbefeuerten Kamin liegen. Sie stammen aus dem 19. Jahrhundert.
Rechts: Vor der bemalten Wandtäfelung hängt eine Auswahl von Ann Shores antiken Saris und gewebten Taschen aus Afrika und Bali. Die marokkanische Truhe – sie bedeckt ein Flokatiteppich – stammt aus dem 19. Jahrhundert. Daneben liegen Stoffe aus Afghanistan und ein Paar Hausschuhe, ebenfalls aus Marokko.

Above: The bed is covered in an Indian patchwork throw and an antique cashmere shawl. In the window hang layers of antique gold lace. The wood chaise longue is by Bruno Mathsson.
Right: Shore uses the light-filled top floor as a showroom for her collection of clothing, textiles and objects.
Facing page: Shore believes that as a Cancerian she has a natural magpie instinct. Above the bed hangs a mobile of assorted jewellery. Of the large gilt mirror she says: "I only like mirrors that are losing their paint."

Ci-dessus: Le lit est recouvert d'un plaid en patchwork indien et d'un châle en cachemire ancien. Devant la fenêtre, des dentelles dorées anciennes. La chaise longue en bois est de Bruno Mathsson.
A droite: Shore utilise le dernier étage, baigné de lumière, pour y exposer sa collection de vêtements, de tissus et d'objets.
Page de droite: Shore pense qu'elle a l'instinct naturel d'une pie. Au-dessus du lit, un mobile fait de bijoux divers et variés. De son miroir doré, elle déclare: «Je n'aime que les miroirs qui s'écaillent».

Oben: Auf dem Bett liegt eine indische Patchwork-Decke und ein alter Schal aus Kashmirwolle. Vor dem Fenster hängen Vorhänge aus alter Goldspitze. Die Chaiselongue aus Holz stammt von Bruno Mathsson.
Rechts: Der lichterfüllte Raum im obersten Stockwerk dient Ann Shore nun als Showroom für ihre Kleidungsstücke, Textilien und Objekte.
Rechte Seite: Ann Shore glaubt einen natürlichen Elster-Instinkt zu besitzen. Über dem Bett hängt ein Mobile aus verschiedenen Schmuckstücken. »Ich mag Spiegel nur, wenn sie blind werden«, kommentiert Ann Shore ihren großen vergoldeten Spiegel.

Below: "There are no magnets on this fridge", Shore announces proudly. Instead it has become a ragged scrapbook of monochromatic inspirational images taken from nature, with door handles entwined in hemp string.
Facing page: Of the kitchen, Shore says: "We don't like anything fitted. We prefer free-standing, functional pieces, it feels more honest." An early 1930s coal-fired Aga provides hot water and cooking facilities, otherwise the only modern convenience is the fridge. There isn't even a television in the house. Instead they live what Shore describes as "a low-key life".

Ci-dessous: «Vous ne verrez pas d'aimants sur ce frigo», annonce fièrement Shore. Au lieu de cela, il est tapissé d'images monochromes s'inspirant de la nature et ses poignées sont ceintes de ficelle en chanvre.
Page de droite: De sa cuisine, Shore déclare: «Je n'aime pas les cuisines équipées. Je préfère les meubles non encastrés, indépendants, fonctionnels, ça me paraît plus honnête.» Un Aga des années 30 alimenté au charbon fournit l'eau chaude et permet de cuisiner. Autrement, le seul autre appareil moderne est le réfrigérateur. Il n'y a même pas de télévision dans la maison. On y mène ce que Shore appelle «une vie humble».

Unten: »Dieser Kühlschrank ist magnetfreie Zone«, bekundet Ann Shore voller Stolz. Stattdessen ist er zu einem Skizzenblock mit inspirierenden, monochromen Bildern geworden, deren Elemente aus der Natur stammen. Die Türgriffe sind mit Hanfseil umwickelt.
Rechte Seite: »Wir mögen eben keine Einbauschränke«, kommentiert Ann Shore ihre Küche. »Frei stehende, funktionelle Teile gefallen uns besser – sie wirken einfach ehrlicher.« Ein kohlenbefeuerter Aga-Herd aus den frühen 1930er Jahren liefert heißes Wasser und Kochmöglichkeiten. Die andere moderne Errungenschaft ist der Kühlschrank. Es gibt nicht einmal einen Fernseher. Stattdessen lebt man hier in Ann Shores Worten ein ruhiges und zurückgezogenes Leben.

Above: The front door is coated with blackboard paint, which Shore has decorated with squiggly white-chalk vine flowers. Every inch of the tall narrow house is brimming with ideas, inspiration, texture and pattern.

Ci-dessus: La porte d'entrée est recouverte d'une peinture pour tableau noir, sur laquelle Shore a gribouillé à la craie des plantes grimpantes. Chaque centimètre carré de la maison regorge d'idées, d'inspiration, de textures et de motifs.

Oben: Die Haustür ist mit einer Farbe beschichtet, die früher für Schultafeln verwendet wurde. Darauf hat Ann Shore in weißer Kreide wildwuchernden Wein gemalt. Jeder Zentimeter ihres schmalen, hohen Hauses quillt förmlich über vor Ideen, Inspirationen, Mustern und unterschiedlichsten Materialien.

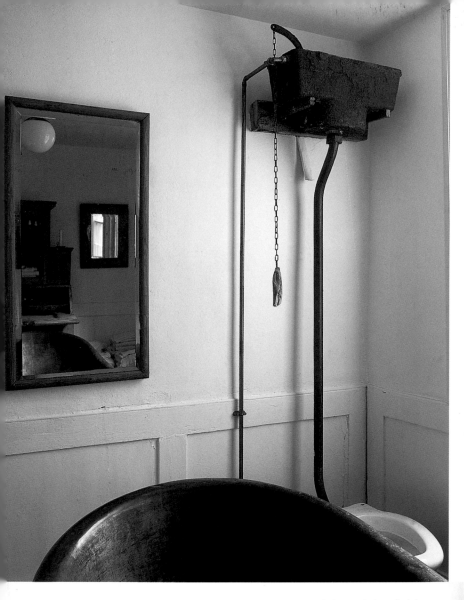

Below: The 19th-century, copper, double-ended, roll-top bath is perfect for two. Rush matting softens the old pine floorboards.

Ci-dessous: On tient facilement à deux dans le haut tub en cuivre aux bords arrondis, qui date du 19ᵉ siècle. Un tapis en jonc évite de se blesser les pieds sur le vieux parquet en sapin.

Unten: Aus dem 19. Jahrhundert stammt die Badewanne aus Kupfer mit sanft geschwungenem Rand. In ihr läßt es sich gut zu zweit baden. Geflochtene Matten machen die alten Fußböden aus Pinienholz etwas fußfreundlicher.

Facing page: The dining room houses an orderly woodpile to fuel the fires on each floor of the house – central heating is an anathema to Shore. Paul Goldman designed the "Cherner" chair in 1957.
Above: The rusty metal cistern was rescued from a local hairdresser's shop and came from the outside toilet. Shore's love of pared-down, functional design is mirrored in the way she chooses to live. Eschewing the luxuries of modern life, she lives quite happily without central heating.

Page de gauche: Dans la salle à manger, des piles de bûches bien ordonnées permettent de faire du feu dans les cheminées à tous les étages. Dans cette maison, le chauffage central serait considéré comme un sacrilège. La chaise «Cherner» de Paul Goldman date de 1957.
Ci-dessus: Le réservoir de chasse d'eau en métal rouillé a été récupéré chez un coiffeur du quartier qui l'avait dans ses latrines au fond de sa cour. Le goût de Shore pour le design dépouillé et fonctionnel se reflète dans son mode de vie. Refusant les luxes du confort moderne, elle se passe très bien de chauffage central.

Linke Seite: Das Brennholz ist sorgfältig im Esszimmer aufgestapelt. Mit diesem Holz werden die Kamine im ganzen Haus versorgt, denn das Wort »Zentralheizung« existiert hier nicht. Paul Goldman entwarf den »Cherner«-Stuhl im Jahr 1957.
Oben: Der rostige Wasserkasten aus Metall wurde aus einem Friseurladen um die Ecke gerettet, wo er zur Außentoilette gehörte. Ann Shore liebt reduziertes, funktionales Design, das ihren Lebensstil widerspiegelt. Auf den Luxus des modernen Lebens kann sie verzichten und ist auch ohne Zentralheizung glücklich.

Brick Lane, London E1

Talvin Singh, lauréat 1999 du «Mercury Prize», la plus prestigieuse des distinctions du monde de la musique, vit depuis huit ans dans une de ces petites rues victoriennes aux maisons toutes identiques, à l'extrême ouest de Londres. Singh est un homme de contrastes, le fruit de l'union entre son Inde ancestrale et une éducation londonienne. S'il est célèbre pour ses créations à l'avant-garde de la musique contemporaine, il a également une solide formation en musique classique indienne. Il a un sens inné de la mode, mêlant le «street style» typiquement londonien et les tenues traditionnelles indiennes. Le décor de sa maison est tout aussi paradoxal. Il a paré son minuscule «cottage» ouvrier traditionnel, deux pièces au rez-de-chaussée, deux pièces à l'étage, des riches couleurs de l'Inde et l'a rempli de meubles, de tissus et d'objets d'Asie. Il aime s'y enfermer, parfois pendant des jours, pour dormir et jouer du tabla. Quand il y est, impossible de le joindre. Il n'a même pas le téléphone et refuse de s'encombrer d'un mobile.

Talvin Singh

Talvin Singh, 1999 winner of the music industry's most prestigious award, the Mercury Prize, has lived in a Victorian terraced house on the outer reaches of East London for the past seven years. Singh is a man of contrasts, a product of his Indian ancestry and East London upbringing. From a classical background he has developed a fusion of western dance and Indian rhythms. His innate fashion sense blends London street style and Indian traditional clothing into an original mix. The décor of his house is no less paradoxical. He has transformed the "two up, two down" Victorian worker's cottage with the rich colours of India and filled it with Asian furniture, textiles and artifacts. He likes to disappear there, sometimes for days on end, to sleep and practise the tabla, and while there he can't be tracked down as there isn't a phone and he refuses to carry a mobile.

Im Jahr 1999 erhielt Talvin Singh einen der prestigeträchtigsten Preise, den die britische Musikindustrie zu vergeben hat: den Mercury Prize. Seit sieben Jahren lebt er in einem viktorianischen Reihenhaus am äußersten Rand von Londons Osten. Talvin Singh ist ein Mann der Gegensätze: von indischer Herkunft, aber aufgewachsen im East End von London. Auch musikalisch verbindet er zwei Persönlichkeiten: die eine steht an vorderster Front der modernen Musik, die andere wurde in klassischer indischer Musik ausgebildet. Sein Gefühl für Mode ist ihm angeboren: eine originelle Mischung aus Londoner »street style« und traditioneller indischer Bekleidung. Nicht weniger paradox ist die Ausstattung seines Hauses. Er hat das traditionelle winzige Reihenhaus, das einst für die Arbeiterklasse konzipiert worden war – oben zwei und unten zwei Räume – mit den intensiven Farben Indiens neu gestaltet und mit Möbeln, Textilien und Artefakten aus Asien angefüllt. Manchmal zieht sich Talvin Singh tagelang hierher zurück und verbringt die Zeit mit Schlafen und dem Tablaspiel. Dann ist er für niemanden zu erreichen, denn das Häuschen hat kein Telefon und Talvin Singh weigert sich, ein Handy bei sich zu tragen.

Previous page: drums from Eastern and Western musical traditions in his Brick Lane studio, designed by Dharmendra Mehta. The lower wall is lined with an evolving artwork – a photocopy collage of cultural and musical inspiration.
Above: "This strong, dark colour is perfect for a practise room. When I wake up, I fall out of bed onto the tablas and start playing."
Right: The living room is dominated by a wall hanging made of embroidered jackets from Punjab.

Page précédente: des tambours traditionnels orientaux et occidentaux dans son studio d'enregistrement de Brick Lane, décoré par Dharmendra Mehta. Le bas du mur est tapissé d'art organique: un collage de photocopies d'inspiration culturelle et musicale.
Ci-dessus: «Cette couleur forte et sombre est idéale pour travailler. Dès mon réveil, je tombe du lit et me mets directement à jouer sur mes tablas.»
A droite: Le salon est dominé par une tenture réalisée à partir de vestes brodées du Pendjab.

Vorhergehende Seite: Schlaginstrumente der östlichen und westlichen Musiktradition haben sich im Studio in Brick Lane angesammelt, das Dharmendra Mehta entworfen hat. Am unteren Teil der Wand hängt ein organisches Kunstwerk, eine Collage aus Fotokopien mit kulturellen und musikalischen Inspirationsquellen.
Oben: »Diese intensive, dunkle Farbe eignet sich perfekt für den Übungsraum. Sobald ich aufwache, falle ich aus dem Bett auf meine Tablas und beginne zu spielen.«
Rechts: Ein Wandbehang, zusammengesetzt aus bestickten Jacken aus dem Pandschab, dominiert das Wohnzimmer.

London Interiors   Talvin Singh

Clockwise from top left: "When I practise, I just have a focus point like a candle in front of me"; compact discs line a diaphanous curtain in the living room; a papier-mâché sculpture of the Indian goddess of music benignly guards a computer in the studio; a prized drum hanging on the wall was a gift from Singh's Indian tabla master.

Du haut à gauche, dans le sens des aiguilles d'une montre: «Lorsque je répète, j'ai besoin de me concentrer sur un point devant moi, comme sur une bougie par exemple»; dans le salon, un rideau diaphane est parsemé de disques compacts; dans le studio, une sculp-

ture en papier mâché représentant la déesse indienne de la musique veille avec bienveillance sur l'ordinateur; le précieux tambourin accroché au mur est un présent du maître de tabla de Singh.

Im Uhrzeigersinn von links oben: »Wenn ich übe, stelle ich vor mir etwas auf, auf das ich mich konzentrieren kann, beispielsweise eine Kerze«; im durchscheinenden Vorhang im Wohnzimmer stecken CDs; die Pappmaché-Skulptur der indischen Göttin der Musik wacht im Studio wohlwollend über einen Computer; die wertvolle Trommel an der Wand war ein Geschenk von Singhs indischem Tablalehrer.

London Interiors   Talvin Singh

Clockwise from top left: Singh's drums are made for him in Bombay; the callus on his left wrist was created by years of pressure on the drums; a statue of the elephant god Ganesha sits on a Victorian marble mantelpiece; Singh's favourite shoes by cult British shoemaker John Moore and a pair of sadhu's wooden sandals.

Du haut à gauche, dans le sens des aiguilles d'une montre: Singh fait faire ses tambours à Bombay; des années de pratique du tambour lui ont laissé ce cal au poignet gauche; une statue de Ganesh, le dieu éléphant, sur un manteau de cheminée victorienne en marbre; les chaussures préférées de Singh, confectionnées par le célèbre chausseur anglais John Moore, et une paire de sandales sadhu en bois.

Im Uhrzeigersinn von links oben: Singhs Trommeln werden eigens für ihn in Bombay gebaut; die Schwiele am Handgelenk ist das Resultat des jahrelangen Trommelspiels; eine Statue der Elefantengottheit Ganesh thront auf einem marmornen Kaminsims aus viktorianischer Zeit; Singhs Lieblingsschuhe stammen vom britischen Schuhmacher John Moore, der Kultstatus erreicht hat. Daneben steht ein Paar indischer Holzsandalen, die dort Sadhus tragen.

Après une période de stagnation dans le design au début des années 1990, de jeunes compagnies innovatrices telles qu'Inflate, créée par Michael Sodeau et deux associés en 1995, ont redonné au secteur apathique la décharge d'adrénaline dont il avait besoin. Inflate a surpris tout le monde avec ses meubles gonflables et, il y a deux ans, Michael Sodeau s'est associé à sa compagne Lisa Giuliani afin d'explorer une gamme de matériaux plus vaste et sortir des limites du plastique gonflable. Ils ont installé le siège de leur nouvelle société dans leur appartement de Highgate aux proportions élégantes. Ce havre de couleurs et de matières neutres, apaisantes et naturelles est l'incarnation d'une décoration tout en retenue et maturité. Toutefois, l'arrivée du petit Oscar a marqué un changement inexorable: le bureau a disparu, cédant la place à l'incontournable collection de jouets en plastique aux couleurs vives, dont certains sont sans nul doute gonflables.

Michael Sodeau & Lisa Giuliani

After the design doldrums of the early 1990s, young innovative companies like Inflate, set up by Michael Sodeau and two partners in 1995, were the necessary jolt of adrenaline needed by a complacent industry. Inflate stormed the fusty cobwebbed scene with its bright plastic blow-up designs. Two years on, Sodeau established a partnership with his girlfriend Lisa Giuliani to explore a larger range of materials outside the limited brief of plastic inflatables. The new company was based in their elegantly proportioned Highgate flat. A haven of soothing neutral colours and natural materials, the apartment is the epitome of restrained, grown-up designer living. However, everything is in an inexorable state of change with the arrival of baby Oscar. Already, the office has gone, making room for Oscar's inevitable collection of brightly coloured plastic toys, some no doubt inflatable.

Nach der Designflaute der frühen 1990er Jahre waren es junge, innovative Firmen wie Inflate, von Michael Sodeau und zwei Partnern im Jahr 1995 gegründet, die der träge und bequem gewordenen Branche den nötigen Adrenalinstoß versetzten. Inflate stürmte die Branche mit einem Blow-up-Design aus Plastik in leuchtenden Farben, und bereits zwei Jahre später gründete Sodeau mit seiner Freundin Lisa Giuliani eine Gesellschaft, um die Produktpalette jenseits der doch begrenzten Möglichkeiten von aufblasbarem Plastik zu erforschen. Diese neue Firma hatte ihren Sitz in der elegant proportionierten, gemeinsamen Wohnung in Highgate. Wie ein schützender Hafen aus beruhigenden, neutralen Farben und natürlichen Materialien ist die Wohnung der Inbegriff zurückhaltenden reifen Designs. Aber alles ist seit der Geburt von Oscar einer unerbittlichen Veränderung unterworfen. Wo vorher das Büro war, ist nun genug Platz für Oscars unvermeidliche Sammlung an Plastikspielzeug in leuchtenden Farben. Ganz bestimmt sind einige von ihnen auch aufblasbar.

Above: Lisa Giuliani at work in the office area of the bedroom, which has now been moved to new premises to accommodate the arrival of Oscar.
Right: The side table is by fellow designer Michael Young. On it sits a vase by Sodeau called "Molar", its design based on a tooth. Behind it, a rosewood standing lamp, designed by Sodeau for the auction house Sotheby's.
Facing page: The furniture throughout the flat is that of Sodeau and his contemporaries, mixed with design classics. Sodeau bought the Jacobsen "Swan" chairs (1957/58) at auction. They came from the Danish Embassy in Holland and still have their original wooden legs.

Ci-dessus: Lisa Giuliani au travail dans le coin bureau de la chambre à coucher qui a à présent disparu.
A droite: Le guéridon est de Michael Young. Dessus, un vase de Sodeau en forme de dent et baptisé, à juste titre, «Molar». Derrière, un luminaire en bois de rose, dessiné par Sodeau pour Sotheby's.
Page de droite: L'appartement est meublé de pièces de Sodeau et de ses contemporains, mélangées avec quelques classiques du design. Sodeau a acheté les chaises «Swan» de Jacobsen (1957/58) dans une vente aux enchères. Elles provenaient de l'ambassade du Danemark en Hollande et ont conservé leur pieds en bois d'origine.

Oben: Lisa Giuliani bei der Arbeit im Bürobereich des Schlafzimmers, das nach der Geburt von Oscar eine neue Funktion erhielt.
Rechts: Den Beistelltisch entwarf Michael Young, darauf steht eine von einem Backenzahn inspirierte Sodeau-Vase namens »Molar«. Die Stehlampe hat Sodeau für das Auktionshaus Sotheby's entworfen.
Rechte Seite: Die ganz Wohnung ist mit Möbeln von Sodeau und seinen Zeitgenossen sowie mit klassischen Designstücken ausgestattet. Arne Jacobsens »Swan«-Stühle (1957/58) erwarb Michael Sodeau bei einer Auktion. Sie besitzen noch die Originalholzbeine.

Cinq semaines après leur rencontre, l'architecte Misha Stefan et sa compagne Yvonne Courtney achetaient cet appartement à l'ouest de Londres. Cela fait aujourd'hui dix ans qu'ils l'occupent. La mezzanine était déjà là, et le reste de l'espace était divisé en petites pièces. Grand admirateur des qualités d'organisation architecturale des termites, Misha Stefan a appliqué les mêmes règles d'ordre en installant ce qu'il appelle un «mur mécanique», à la fois vitrine et placard, qui accueille tout et n'importe quoi, de la machine à laver à des livres et de la porcelaine. Le vestibule est compact, mais tout aussi bien organisé et conçu dans une économie d'espace. Stefan est parvenu à y caser des toilettes, des placards pour les divers compteurs et même une petite alcôve où l'on range les clefs de l'entrée. Se décrivant comme un «moderniste soft», Stefan a créé un style moins austère, plus fluide et organique que le modernisme pur et dur, tout en conservant un sens de l'ordre et de la fonctionnalité.

Misha Stefan & Yvonne Courtney

Five weeks after they first met, architect Misha Stefan and his partner Yvonne Courtney bought this flat in West London – that was ten years ago. It already had the mezzanine floor, while the rest of the space was divided into smaller rooms. Professing an admiration for the organised architectural skills of termites, Stefan has brought a similar sense of order to his home by installing what he calls "a mechanical wall", which combines display and practicality, housing everything from the washing machine to china and books. The entrance hall is compact, but just as organised and space-saving, managing to fit in a loo, a cupboard for the utility meters and even a special alcove to hold the front-door keys. Describing himself as a "soft modernist", he achieves a look that is less austere, more fluid and organic than pure Modernism, while still retaining its sense of order and functionality.

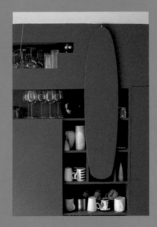

Fünf Wochen, nachdem sie sich kennen gelernt hatten, kauften der Architekt Misha Stefan und seine Partnerin Yvonne Courtney diese Wohnung im Westen Londons. Das war vor zehn Jahren. Damals existierte schon das Zwischengeschoss; der Rest der Wohnung war in kleinere Räume unterteilt. Misha Stefan bewundert die Bauten der gut organisierten Termiten und hat versucht, die Wohnung entsprechend zu ordnen. Dazu verwendete er »mechanische Wände« wie er sie selbst nennt, in denen sich Dinge ausstellen oder praktisch verstauen lassen – ob es nun die Waschmaschine ist, das Porzellan oder die Bücher. Der Eingangsbereich ist kompakt und dennoch Raum sparend organisiert. Hier finden sogar eine Toilette, ein Schrank für Gas- und Stromzähler und eine Nische für die Haustürschlüssel Platz. Misha Stefan beschreibt sich selbst als »soften Modernisten«, und tatsächlich wirkt die Wohnung nicht karg, sondern hat etwas Fließendes und Organisches. Dennoch bleibt das Gefühl von Ordnung und Funktionalität erhalten.

Below: Stefan designed the voluptuously shaped, free-standing, mosaic pedestal basin in the bathroom.
Facing page: Stefan's admiration for the Spanish architect Antoni Gaudí is most apparent in the kitchen, with its ergonomically designed cooking and sink islands. Ingeniously, the electric circular hobs are arranged in a line, such an obvious way to avoid possible burns to the arm that it is extraordinary that all electric cookers aren't designed like this. The island has in-built storage for knives and utensils, and above it hangs a light switch weighted with a fisherman's lead.

Ci-dessous: Misha Stefan a dessiné l'élégant lavabo en mosaïque de la salle de bains.
Page de droite: C'est dans la cuisine, avec ses îlots indépendants pour la cuisinière et l'évier, que l'on ressent le plus l'admiration de Stefan pour l'architecte catalan Antoni Gaudí. Les plaques chauffantes sont alignées, ce qui évite de se brûler, un détail si ingénieux qu'on se demande pourquoi on n'y avait pas pensé plus tôt. Les îlots sont équipés d'espaces de rangement pour les couverts et les ustensiles de cuisine. Au-dessus de l'îlot central, un interrupteur de chalutier suspendu au bout d'un fil à plomb.

Unten: Das frei stehende elegant geschwungene Mosaik-Waschbecken im Badezimmer ist ein Entwurf von Misha Stefan.
Rechte Seite: Stefans Bewunderung für den spanischen Architekten Antoni Gaudí ist in der Küche mit ihren ergonomisch gestalteten Koch- und Spülinseln am augenfälligsten. Wirklich gut ist die Idee, die elektrischen Herdplatten nebeneinander anzuordnen, sodass man sich beim Darüberreichen nicht verbrennen kann, und man fragt sich, warum nicht alle Herde so konzipiert sind. Die Kochinsel verfügt über eingebaute Stauflächen für Messer und Küchenutensilien. Von der Decke hängt ein Senkblei, das hier nicht zum Fischen, sondern zum Anschalten des Lichts verwendet wird.

Above: On the mezzanine floor, the bathroom is reached from the bedroom area through a wide gold-painted swivel door. When angled just right, the door allows Yvonne to "do her boudoir behind it, while I can be left in peace to do my teeth," says Stefan.
Previous pages: Stefan describes himself as a "soft modernist", which presumably allows him to incorporate soft furnishings, decorative elements, colour and even a touch of clutter into their home with a clear conscience.

Ci-dessus: Sur la mezzanine, on accède à la salle de bains depuis la chambre en passant par une large porte pivotante peinte en or. Lorsque la porte est ouverte à un certain angle, «Yvonne peut se maquiller d'un côté, pendant que je me brosse tranquillement les dents de l'autre», explique Stefan.
Double page précédente: Stefan se décrit lui-même comme un «moderniste soft», ce qui lui permet d'utiliser des tissus, des éléments décoratifs, de la couleur et même une touche de désordre dans la maison tout en gardant la conscience tranquille.

Oben: Das Badezimmer im Zwischengeschoss erreicht man über eine breite, gold gestrichene Drehtür im Schlafbereich. Wenn die Tür genau im richtigen Winkel ausgerichtet ist, »kann Yvonne sich schminken und ich mir in Ruhe auf der anderen Seite die Zähne putzen«, erklärt Stefan.
Vorhergehende Doppelseite: Als »soften Modernisten« beschreibt sich Misha Stefan selbst. Diese Definition erlaubt es ihm, ohne schlechtes Gewissen weiche Stoffe, dekorative Details, Farben und sogar einen Hauch von Unordnung in seiner Wohnung zu vereinen.

Westbourne Grove, London W11

Apparu dans les années 1990, le phénomène du «stylisme floral» a incontestablement trouvé son chef de meute en la personne de Nikki Tibbles, propriétaire de Wild at Heart. Sa liste de clients comprend tous les magasins les plus chic de Bond Street. Sa boutique et son kiosque de Notting Hill sont aussi célèbres pour leur architecture que pour leurs somptueux bouquets. Future Systems, un cabinet d'architectes primé, est responsable du décor organique bleu glacé de sa boutique, comme de l'appartement qu'elle partage avec son compagnon Oliver Backhouse. Ils habitent deux étages baignés de lumière, tout en bois blanc et blond et aménagés avec une sélection soignée de meubles classiques et modernes du 20ᵉ siècle. Tibbles, que l'on soupçonne d'être, au fond d'elle-même, une fille de la campagne, y a ajouté sa propre touche de chaos et de confusion avec l'aide de ses deux amies à quatre pattes, Maizie et Rosie, qui batifolent joyeusement dans l'appartement.

Nikki Tibbles

The phenomenon of the "designer" florist emerged in the 1990s and today Nikki Tibbles of Wild at Heart is arguably the leader of the pack. Her client list includes all of Bond Street's most fashionable emporiums and her Notting Hill shop and flower stall are noted as much for their architectural design as for the gorgeous blooms on display. The award-winning practice Future Systems was responsible for the ice-blue organic architecture of the shop as well as for the home she shares with partner Oliver Backhouse. The flat is a clean, white and blonde wood, light-filled space over two floors, filled with a restrained selection of contemporary and classic 20th-century furnishings. Tibbles, who one suspects is a country girl at heart, adds a big dash of chaos and confusion into the mix in the form of her two canine friends Maizie and Rosie, who gambol around enthusiastically.

Das Phänomen des »Designerfloristen« entwickelte sich im vergangenen Jahrzehnt. Heute ist Nikki Tibbles von Wild at Heart sicherlich die führende unter ihnen. Auf ihrer Kundenliste stehen die prominentesten Modehäuser der Bond Street, und ihr Geschäft sowie ihr Blumenstand in Notting Hill sind wegen ihrer Architektur und ihrer hinreißenden Blütenpracht mindestens genauso bekannt. Für die Architektur – eisblau-organisch – zeichnet das preisgekrönte Designbüro Future Systems verantwortlich, das das Geschäft und auch das Zuhause von Nikki gestaltete, das sie mit ihrem Partner Oliver Backhouse teilt. Die gemeinsame Wohnung wirkt freundlich – weißes und helles Holz, lichterfüllte Räume, die sich über zwei Etagen erstrecken und mit einer Sammlung zurückhaltenden, zeitgenössischen und klassischen Designs aus dem 20. Jahrhundert möbliert sind. Dennoch wird man das Gefühl nicht los, dass Nikki Tibbles im Herzen ein richtiges Mädchen vom Land ist. Überall hinterlässt sie einen gehörigen Schuss an Chaos – in Form ihrer beiden Freunde, der Hündinnen Maizie und Rosie, die wild umhertollen.

Previous page: Tibbles and Maizie nestled together in an Arne Jacobsen "Egg" chair in the living room.
Clockwise from top left: view of the kitchen; objects on display: the etchings are by Oliver's stepfather, Jeremy Fraser; Maizie is a Rhodesian Ridgeback cross; the gas fire has a layer of pebbles.

Page précédente: dans le salon, Tibbles et Maizie blotties dans un fauteuil «Egg» d'Arne Jacobsen.
Du haut à gauche, dans le sens des aiguilles d'une montre: la cuisine; des objets exposés sur un buffet; les gravures sont de Jeremy Fraser, le beau-père d'Oliver; Maizie est le fruit d'un croisement avec un Rhodesian Ridgeback; la cheminée à gaz est tapissée de galets.

Vorhergehende Doppelseite: Nikki und Maisie kuscheln zusammen in Arne Jacobsens »Egg«-Sessel im Wohnzimmer.
Im Uhrzeigersinn von links oben: Blick auf die Küche; verschiedene Objekte: Die Radierungen stammen von Olivers Stiefvater Jeremy Fraser; Maizie ist eine Rhodesian-Ridgeback-Mischlingshündin; das Gasfeuer im Kamin wird von Kieselsteinen eingefasst.

London Interiors　　　　Nikki Tibbles

Nikki asked Angus Pond from Future Systems to create "a sense of space and light" in what was previously six rooms over two floors. Nikki and her partner, Oliver, have opted for selected pieces of classic 20th-century furniture, including Mies van der Rohe "Barcelona" chairs, Arne Jacobsen moulded-plywood "Series 7" chairs and a Knoll "Tulip" table.

Nikki a demandé à Angus Pond, de Future Systems, de créer une «impression d'espace et de lumière» dans ce qui était auparavant six pièces réparties sur deux étages. Avec son compagnon Oliver, ils ont

opté pour des classiques du mobilier du 20ᵉ siècle dont les fauteuils «Barcelona» de Mies van der Rohe, les chaises en contreplaqué moulé «Series 7» d'Arne Jacobsen et une table «Tulip» de Knoll.

»Ein Gefühl von Raum und Licht zu schaffen« in einer Wohnung, die vorher aus sechs Zimmern auf zwei Etagen bestand – das war die Anweisung von Nikki Tibbles an Angus Pond von Future Systems. Das Paar entschied sich für Designklassiker des 20. Jahrhunderts, wie Mies van der Rohes »Barcelona«-Stühle, Arne Jacobsens »Series 7«-Stühle aus geformtem Schichtholz und ein »Tulip«-Tisch der Firma Knoll.

Nikki refers to the lower-floor living area as "the snuggy" room. The fake fur cushions are often spread out over the floor for watching TV, but Oliver's Charles and Ray Eames rosewood and leather "Lounge chair" and ottoman is undoubtedly the top spot. Between the books is a group of coloured Perspex vases from Space.

Nikki appelle le séjour du premier étage son «nid». Les coussins en fausse fourrure sont souvent étalés sur le sol pour regarder la télévision, mais la chaise longue en bois de rose et cuir de Charles et Ray Eames,

qui appartient à Oliver, est indubitablement le meilleur endroit. Entre les livres, un groupe de vases colorés en Perspex de Space.

Die untere Wohnetage nennt Nikki Tibbles den »Kuschelbereich«. Beim Fernsehen werden die Kissen aus Kunstpelz oft überall auf dem Boden verstreut. Herzstück ist sicherlich der »Lounge chair« mit passendem Hocker aus Rosenholz und Leder, entworfen von Charles und Ray Eames. Zwischen den Büchern stehen bunte Perspex-Vasen von Space.

Clockwise from top left: *view from the podlike bathroom, which is open on two sides and has curved sliding doors; the double-ended bed is centrally placed in the sleeping area; looking through the bathroom pod to the bed area – the floors on this level are birch ply; Rosie, who is "pure mutt", reclines on Nikki's silk quilt.*

Du haut à gauche, dans le sens des aiguilles d'une montre: *une vue depuis la salle de bains tout en courbes qui est ouverte sur deux côtés et équipée de portes coulissantes incurvées; le lit à deux têtes est placé au centre du coin chambre à coucher; vue depuis la salle de bains vers*
le coin chambre, où le plancher est en bouleau; Rosie, «corniaud pure race» est couchée sur l'édredon en soie de Nikki.

Im Uhrzeigersinn von links oben: *Blick aus dem wie ein Gehäuse entworfenen Badezimmer, das an zwei Seiten offen ist und über konvex geformte Schiebetüren verfügt; das Bett mit zwei Kopfteilen ist in der Mitte des Schlafbereichs platziert; Blick aus dem Badezimmer-»Gehäuse« auf den Schlafbereich mit Böden aus Birkenholz; »Typisch Köter« – Madame Rosie macht es sich auf dem Seidenquilt von Frauchen bequem.*

Charterhouse Street, London EC1

Le travail et la maison du photographe Wolfgang Tillmans offrent un antidote apaisant à l'obsession du style et de la griffe qui marque notre époque. Tandis que le passe-temps préféré de nombreux Londoniens est la chasse aux pièces rares signées Aalto, Eames ou Panton, Tillmans préfère s'entourer de meubles de bureau simples et fonctionnels. Il habite au dernier étage d'un sinistre immeuble de bureaux dans un endroit sans caractère entre Clerkenwell, le nouveau quartier à la mode, et le Bloomsbury endormi. Après avoir vécu épisodiquement à Londres pendant neuf ans, Tillmans n'a finalement décidé de séparer son lieu de travail de son lieu d'habitation que l'année dernière. Pour lui, « Le loft va à l'encontre de la nature humaine. C'est trop ouvert. Je n'aime pas avoir 200 mètres de vide devant moi quand je suis couché dans mon lit ni entendre le fax sonner toute la nuit ». Son atelier se trouve désormais à quinze minutes en bicyclette, dans un bâtiment d'usine de Bethnal Green tout aussi insignifiant. Là, Tillmans poursuit son art, qui consiste à extraire la beauté du quelconque.

Wolfgang Tillmans

In our style-conscious and label-obsessed age, the work and home of photographer Wolfgang Tillmans provide a refreshing antidote. While hunting down rare pieces by Aalto, Eames or Panton has become an obsessional pastime for many Londoners, Tillmans prefers to surround himself with plain, functional office furniture. His home is equally anonymous – the top floor of a dreary office building in a nondescript tract of the city between newly fashionable Clerkenwell and sedate Bloomsbury. Tillmans has lived in London off and on for the past nine years and finally separated his work and living accommodation last year. For him, "The loft thing is against human nature. It is too open. I didn't like lying in bed with 200 metres in front of me and the fax machine going off all night." His studio is now a 15-minute bicycle ride away in an equally anonymous Bethnal Green factory building. Here Tillmans pursues his idiosyncratic art – drawing out beauty from the mundane.

In unserer so stil- und markenbewußten Zeit wirkt die Arbeit und das Zuhause des Fotografen Wolfgang Tillmans wie ein erfrischendes Kontrastprogramm. Während viele Londoner geradezu besessen nach seltenen Stücken von Alvar Aalto, dem Ehepaar Eames oder Verner Panton jagen, zieht Wolfgang Tillmans schlichte, funktionale Büromöbel vor. Sein Zuhause ist ähnlich sachlich – gelegen im obersten Stockwerk eines durchschnittlichen Bürogebäudes zwischen dem inzwischen populär gewordenen Clerkenwell und dem gediegenen Bloomsbury, in einer völlig unauffälligen Ecke der Stadt. Schon seit neun Jahren lebt Tillmans mit Unterbrechungen in London. Erst im vergangenen Jahr zog er einen Trennstrich zwischen Wohn- und Arbeitsbereich. »Dieses Loftleben verstößt doch gegen die menschliche Natur«, meint er. »Es ist einfach zu offen. Mir jedenfalls gefiel es nicht, im Bett zu liegen und vor mir 200 Meter Platz zu haben und die ganze Nacht das Fax zu hören.« Jetzt liegt sein Studio eine Viertelstunde mit dem Fahrrad entfernt, in einem ebenso unauffälligen Fabrikgebäude in Bethnal Green. Hier geht Tillmans seiner sensiblen Kunst nach, aus der Banalität des Lebens die Schönheit zu filtern.

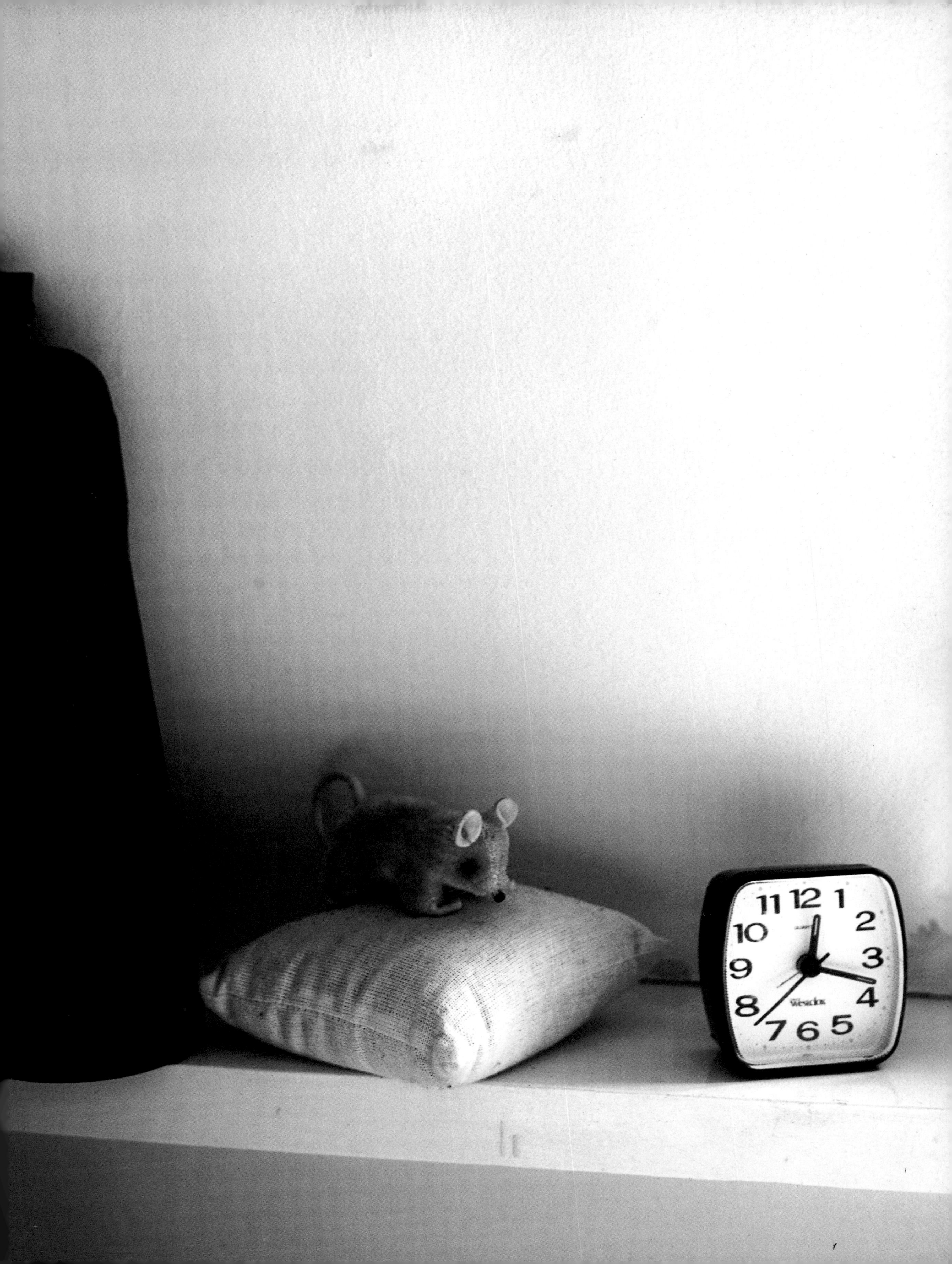

Clockwise from top left: the top-floor living space with anonymous practical furniture bought from local office-supply stores; a pile of autumn leaves lying in the entrance hall; against the wall stands a photograph by Tillmans; Tillmans is unsure about the blonde-wood chairs from Habitat and table from Pesch, feeling that "They are too designer 1990s, too easy to label."

Du haut à gauche, dans le sens des aiguilles d'une montre: l'appartement, au dernier étage de l'immeuble, et les meubles anonymes et pratiques achetés dans un magasin de fournitures de bureau local;

un tas de feuilles d'automne dans un coin de l'entrée; au mur, une photographie de Tillmans; Tillmans n'est pas très satisfait de ses chaises Habitat et de sa table Pesch en bois blond.

Im Uhrzeigersinn von links oben: Der Wohnbereich im obersten Stockwerk ist mit unauffälligen, praktischen Möbeln eingerichtet, die bei Büroausstattern aus dem Viertel erworben wurden; Herbstblätter häufen sich im Eingangsbereich; an der Wand lehnt ein Tillmans-Foto; so ganz sicher ist er sich bei den furnierten Sperrholzstühlen von Habitat und dem Tisch von Pesch noch nicht.

London Interiors   Wolfgang Tillmans

Clockwise from top left: In the studio, cacti are among the mundane, often unappealing objects that Tillmans' work draws our attention to; a crate is now a display table for a vegetable still life; a veneered boardroom conference table and metal garment storage bins left by the previous tenants; the doors to the mens' and ladies' toilets remain from the studio's previous incarnation as a clothing factory.

Du haut à gauche, dans le sens des aiguilles d'une montre: Les cactus font partie de ces objets banals sur lesquels Tillmans aime attirer notre attention; une caisse est convertie en console; une table de confé-rence en placage de bois et des étagères laissées par les précédents loca-taires; les portes de toilettes pour dames et messieurs sont un souvenir de la précédente incarnation des locaux, un atelier de confection.

Im Uhrzeigersinn von links oben: Das Stillleben ist ein Beispiel für die banalen Objekte, auf die Tillmans uns in seinen Arbeiten aufmerksam macht; eine Transportkiste dient als Dekoauslagefläche; den großen Konferenztisch und die Metallboxen hat der frühere Mieter zurückgelassen; die Toilettentüren sind noch Überbleibsel aus dem früheren Leben des jetzigen Studios als Kleiderfabrik.

Previous pages: The studio originally belonged to a furrier. Security bars cage the windows, while ominous lengths of wire criss-cross the ceiling – once they would have been electrified.
Above: The lounge area is furnished with office chairs – "Very Prada" says Tillmans, tongue in cheek – and with hardwood seamstresses' benches, left by the previous occupants.
Right: The blue velour three-piece suite was bought by Tillmans' parents when they were newlyweds in the early 1960s.
Following pages: details from around the kitchen and lounge.

Double page précédente: A l'origine, l'atelier abritait un fourreur. Les fenêtres sont équipées de barreaux et l'inquiétant quadrillage métallique au plafond était autrefois électrifié.
Ci-dessus: Le coin salon est meublé de fauteuils de bureau, «très Prada» dit Tillmans avec ironie, et de bancs de couturières en bois dur laissés par les précédents occupants des lieux.
A droite: Le salon en velours bleu a été acheté par les parents de Tillmans dans les années 1960 quand ils étaient jeunes mariés.
Double page suivante: détails de la cuisine et du coin salon.

Vorhergehende Doppelseite: Früher war hier eine Kürschnerei untergebracht. Man sieht noch die Sicherheitsgitter am Fenster.
Oben: Die Sitzecke ist mit Bürosesseln – »wie bei Prada« meint Tillmans ironisch – und den Hartholz-Sitzbänken der Näherinnen ausgestattet.
Rechts: Die dreiteilige Sitzgruppe aus blauem Velours erwarben die Eltern von Tillmans kurz nach ihrer Heirat Anfang der 1960er Jahre.
Folgende Doppelseite: Details aus der Küche und der Sitzecke.

London Interiors   Wolfgang Tillmans

Le samedi soir qui précéda la mort tragique de la princesse Diana, Margaret Tyler regardait une vidéo de son mariage de conte de fées en compagnie de quelques amis. Pour quelqu'un d'autre, cela n'aurait été qu'une coïncidence étrange, mais dans le cas de Tyler, il aurait été encore plus bizarre qu'il en soit autrement. Surnommée la plus «Loyaliste des Royalistes» par les tabloïdes britanniques, Margaret Tyler a commencé il y a 22 ans ce qui est sans doute la plus grande collection au monde de bibelots aux effigies de la couronne, en achetant un petit plat en verre pour 2 pences 1/2. Une des pièces de sa maison en faux style Tudor dans le nord de Wembley est vite devenue «la chambre royale», territoire interdit pour ses quatre bambins en bas âge. A mesure que les enfants ont quitté le nid familial, la collection a augmenté pour prendre leur place. Les week-ends, la demeure se convertit en bed & breakfast pour accueillir d'autres passionnés. Ils peuvent choisir parmi plusieurs petits déjeuners aux noms royaux. Naturellement, le «prince Andrew» est le plus British et le plus copieux.

Margaret Tyler

On the Saturday night before Princess Diana's shocking death, Margaret Tyler was watching a video of the Princess' fairy-tale wedding with a few like-minded friends. If this had been anyone else, it would perhaps have been an eerily ironic coincidence, but in Tyler's case it would possibly have been more bizarre if she had not. Dubbed the "Loyalist of Royalists" by the British tabloids, Tyler started what must surely be the largest collection of Royal memorabilia in the world 22 years ago with the purchase of a small glass dish for 2 1/2 pence. One room of her 1930s mock-Tudor house in North Wembley quickly became the "Royal Room" and out of bounds to her four small children. As the children have grown up and left home, the collection has grown to take their place. At weekends she fills her extra bedrooms with fellow enthusiasts on a bed & breakfast basis. They can choose from a range of royally titled breakfast dishes – the Prince Andrew is "a full English", of course.

Am Samstagabend vor Prinzessin Dianas tragischem Unfall hatte sich Margaret Tyler mit einigen »Gleichgesinnten« das Video von der Märchenhochzeit der Prinzessin angesehen. Bei jedem anderen hätte man das als gespenstischen Zufall gewertet. Bei Margaret Tyler hingegen wäre das Gegenteil bizarrer gewesen, denn sie gilt als königlicher als die Königsfamilie und wurde von den englischen Massenblättern »Loyalist of the Royalists« getauft. Margaret Tyler besitzt die wohl weltweit größte Sammlung zum Thema britisches Königshaus. Den Grundstein dafür legte sie vor 22 Jahren mit dem Erwerb eines kleinen Glastellers zum Preis von 2 1/2 pence. Rasch avancierte ein Zimmer ihres im Tudorstil gehaltenen Hauses in North Wembley – das allerdings aus den 1930er Jahren stammt – zum »Königszimmer«, das ihre vier kleinen Kinder nicht betreten durften. Jetzt, da die Kinder erwachsen und aus dem Haus sind, nimmt die königliche Sammlung deren Platz ein. An den Wochenenden lädt Margaret Tyler Gleichgesinnte zum »bed and breakfast« ein und bietet zum Frühstück eine Auswahl königlicher Gerichte. Dass das »Prince Andrew« ein »full English breakfast« ist, versteht sich von selbst.

Previous pages: The house was built in the 1930s as part of a large suburban estate in North Wembley. Margaret Tyler is known to film crews and international magazines and makes regular media appearances.

Right and below: Tyler acquired many of her larger pieces from the Royal exhibition in Windsor that was dismantled a few years ago. She got other things, including the large Union Jacks that cover her chairs and sofa from the weekly market at Covent Garden on Mondays. "I can't imagine living in a place with plain walls. People ask me where I live; I live right in the middle of it."

Double page précédente: La maison a été construite dans les années 1930 sur un vaste domaine au nord de Wembley. Bien connue des équipes de tournage et de la presse internationale, Margaret Tyler apparaît régulièrement dans les médias.

A droite et ci-dessous: Tyler a acheté une grande partie de ses pièces les plus imposantes il y a quelques années lors du démontage de l'exposition royale de Windsor. D'autres pièces, comme les grands Unions Jacks qui recouvrent le canapé et les fauteuils, proviennent du marché qui se tient tous les lundis à Covent Garden. «Je ne peux pas m'imaginer dans une maison aux murs nus. On me demande souvent où je vis: Ici, au beau milieu de tout ça!»

Vorhergehende Doppelseite: Das Haus wurde in den 1930er Jahren im Norden des Vororts Wembley errichtet. Margaret Tyler ist regelmäßig im Fernsehen und in internationalen Zeitschriften zu sehen.

Rechts und unten: Viele der größeren Stücke in ihrer Sammlung erstand sie auf der vor einigen Jahren aufgelösten Königlichen Ausstellung in Windsor. Andere Exponate, wie den großen Union Jack, der auf den Sesseln und dem Sofa drapiert ist, erwarb sie montags auf dem Wochenmarkt in Covent Garden. »In einer Wohnung mit leeren Wänden zu leben – das könnte ich nicht. Die Leute fragen mich oft, wo ich hier überhaupt lebe; ich lebe einfach mittendrin.«

The house is arranged chronologically, starting with Queen Victoria in
the converted garage and includes areas and rooms dedicated to the
Coronation, the Jubilee and various members of the family. There is a
corner for Princess Anne, Edward and Sophie are in the hall, Andrew
and Fergie are by the stairs and the Queen Mother gets a whole room
as does Princess Diana and the Queen. Tyler doesn't drive so has to
hire a van to pick up larger items. However, she was able to carry the
black and white Prince Charles cutout home on the Tube.

La maison est aménagée chronologiquement, à commencer par la
reine Victoria qui occupe l'ancien garage. Certaines parties, voire des
pièces entières, sont consacrées au Couronnement, au Jubilé et à certains membres de la famille royale. La princesse Anne a son petit coin.
Edward et Sophie sont dans le couloir. Andrew et Fergie ont l'escalier.
La reine mère a droit à sa propre pièce, tout comme la princesse
Diana et la reine. Tyler ne conduisant pas, elle loue les services de dé-
ménageurs pour aller chercher ses objets les plus volumineux. Néanmoins, elle a pu transporter par métro le prince Charles en carton noir
et blanc.

Die Ausstellung ist chronologisch angeordet. Es beginnt in der umge-
bauten Garage mit Königin Victoria; eigene Räume und Bereiche sind
der Krönung von Königin Elizabeth II. und ihrer Goldenen Hochzeit
gewidmet. Prinzessin Anne hat ihre Ecke, Edward und Sophie sind in
der Eingangshalle, Andrew und Fergie nahe der Treppe. Die Königin-
mutter hat ihr eigenes Zimmer – so auch Prinzessin Diana und die
Königin. Da Margaret Tyler selbst nicht Auto fährt, lässt sie größere
Stücke von einem Umzugswagen transportieren. Den schwarzweißen
Aufsteller von Prinz Charles hat sie allerdings selbst in der U-Bahn
nach Hause transportiert.

Left and below: Tyler has worked for the Downs Syndrome Association. She takes 27 days off work a year and uses those days to follow members of the Royal Family on official visits or to visit various Royal exhibitions or houses. The crown displayed on the throne was a gift from Jeanette Charles, a Queen look-a-like.
Facing page: the "Diana room".
Following pages, clockwise from top left: Tyler always wears red, white and blue for her Royal visits; the breakfast table is always laid with a selection of Royal teapots, and Charles and Diana egg cups; a "Prince William" doll; the corgis in the "Queen Mother room" came from a friend in Bradford.

Ci-dessus et à droite: Tyler a travaillé pour l'association des enfants trisomiques. Elle s'octroie 27 jours de congé par an afin de suivre les membres de la famille royale dans des visites officielles et pour visiter des expositions ou des demeures royales. La couronne exposée sur le trône est un don de Jeanette Charles, un sosie de la reine.
Page de droite: la « Diana Room ».
Double page suivante, du haut à gauche dans le sens des aiguilles d'une montre: Lors de ses visites royales, Tyler s'habille toujours en rouge, bleu et blanc ; la table du petit déjeuner est toujours dressée avec un assortiment de théières royales et de coquetiers « Charles et Diana » ; une poupée « William » ; les corgis dans la « Chambre de la reine mère » viennent d'une amie de Bradford.

Oben und rechts: Tyler war für die Downs Syndrome Association tätig, dem englischen Interessenverband für Menschen mit Downs-Syndrom. 27 Tage Urlaub nimmt sie im Jahr, um Mitglieder des Königshauses auf offiziellen Besuchen zu begleiten oder entsprechende Ausstellungen oder Häuser zu besichtigen. Die Krone auf dem Thron war ein Geschenk von Jeanette Charles, einer Doppelgängerin der Queen.
Rechte Seite: der »Diana Room«.
Folgende Doppelseite, im Uhrzeigersinn von oben links: Bei königlichen Besuchen trägt Margaret Tyler grundsätzlich Rot, Weiss und Blau; der Frühstückstisch ist immer mit einer Sammlung königlicher Teekannen und Eierbechern mit Charles & Diana-Motiven gedeckt; eine Prinz-William-Puppe; die Corgis im »Queen Mother Room« sind ein Geschenk einer Freundin aus Bradford.

Pour un homme d'affaires qui vit dans ses valises en sautant d'un grand hôtel international à un autre, l'achat de cet appartement à Marylebone était un choix particulièrement judicieux. Perché au dernier étage d'un immeuble de la fin des années 1960, il est surmonté de terrasses d'où l'on jouit d'une vue spectaculaire sur la ville. Ian Chee, de chez VX Design, chargé d'aménager l'intérieur, n'en revient toujours pas. En effet, originaire de Singapour, Chee est habitué aux entassements verticaux des métropoles du sud-est asiatique, où même habiter au 40ᵉ étage ne garantit pas un panorama dégagé. Si les charmes potentiels de la vue et du jardin suspendu de l'appartement étaient immédiatement perceptibles, ses plafonds bas et ses pièces carrées étaient d'une horizontalité oppressante. Chee a donc cherché à l'aérer en créant une impression de loft. L'ouverture pratiquée dans le plafond de la salle de séjour en L, les lignes courbes de l'escalier métallique en colimaçon et le bureau en grande partie vitré qui chapeaute le tout attirent le regard vers le haut.

Urban Oasis

For a businessman used to living out of a suitcase in top international hotels, the purchase of this Marylebone flat seems particularly appropriate. Perched on the top floor of a late-1960s block with terraces above, the apartment enjoys spectacular city views. Ian Chee of VX Design, who was commissioned to transform the interior, marvels at its location: "It's only on the eighth floor, but you can't imagine how beautiful it is." Chee, who is Singaporean, is used to the crowded vertical spaces of modern Asian cities, where even living on the 40th floor doesn't guarantee an uninterrupted view. The potential charms of the flat's outlook and roof garden were immediate, but low ceilings and boxy rooms made the living space feel oppressively horizontal. Chee's brief was to open it out to create a "lofty feeling". A void inserted into the L-shaped living room, the lines of the metal circular staircase and the semi-glazed study pavilion above all draw the eye upwards.

Zu einem Geschäftsmann, der es gewohnt ist, aus dem Koffer zu leben und in den besten Hotels abzusteigen, passt der Kauf dieser Wohnung im Stadtteil Marylebone besonders gut. Auf dem obersten Stockwerk eines Häuserblocks aus den späten 1960er Jahren thronend, bietet sie von der Terrasse aus einen atemberaubenden Blick auf die Stadt. Ian Chee von VX Design hatte den Auftrag, die Wohnung umzugestalten, und war von der Location schier begeistert: »Es ist zwar nur der achte Stock, aber unvorstellbar schön.« Der das sagt, stammt allerdings auch aus Singapur und ist an die beengten hohen Räume moderner asiatischer Städte gewöhnt, wo selbst im 40. Stock ein unverbauter Blick nicht selbstverständlich ist. Die Vorzüge der Wohnung – der Blick und der Terrassengarten – waren augenscheinlich. Da die niedrigen Decken und schachtelförmigen Räume dem Wohnbereich jedoch etwas bedrückend Horizontales verliehen, sollte Ian Chee die Räume öffnen, um ein »Loft-Gefühl« zu schaffen. Er durchbrach in dem L-förmigen Wohnzimmer die Decke und setzte eine Wendeltreppe ein, die den Blick automatisch nach oben lenkt, hinauf zu dem teilverglasten Pavillon, der als Arbeitszimmer dient.

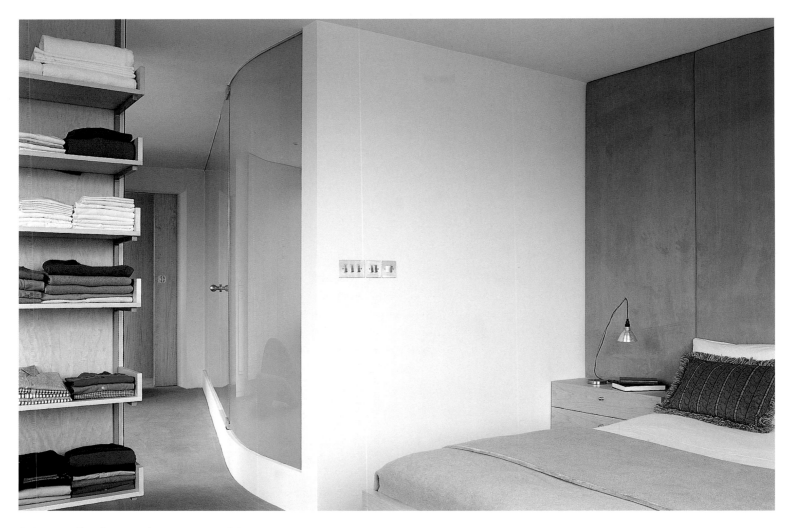

Facing page: The client wanted a steam room and shower, not a bath, in his bathroom. Enclosed by a curved sandblasted glass wall, the room is lined in marble.
Above: In the main bedroom, sycamore wood shelving floats 20 centimetres above the floor and beyond is the dressing area and shower steam room.
Right: The oxblood calfskin bedhead with lightbox and shelf behind is the dominant feature in the second bedroom.

Page de gauche: Pour sa salle de bains, le client ne voulait pas de baignoire mais d'un hammam et d'une douche. Fermée d'un côté par une paroi arrondie en verre dépoli, la pièce est tapissée de marbre.
Ci-dessus: Dans la chambre principale, des étagères en sycomore flottent à 20 centimètres au-dessus du sol. Au fond, on aperçoit le dressing et le mur du hammam.
A droite: La seconde chambre à coucher est dominée par une tête de lit en veau teint «sang de bœuf», avec un éclairage et des étagères intégrés.

Linke Seite: Der Kunde wollte in seinem Badezimmer keine Badewanne, sondern Dampfbad und Dusche. Der Raum wird durch eine gebogene, gesandstrahlte Glaswand abgetrennt und ist mit Marmor ausgekleidet.
Oben: Im großen Schlafzimmer hängen Regale aus Amerikanischem Bergahorn 20 Zentimeter über dem Boden. Dahinter liegen der Ankleidebereich und das Duschdampfbad.
Rechts: Im zweiten Schlafzimmer ist das Kopfteil aus ochsenblutrotem Kalbsleder bestimmendes Element. Leuchtkasten und Regal sind dahinter angebracht.

L'influence du minimalisme pur et dur des années 1980 a longtemps voulu que les luminaires soient les plus discrets possibles, sinon complètement cachés. Puis, il y a quelques années, est apparu un très pittoresque «abat-jour emballé dans de la soie». Conçu par Peter Wylly, de Babylon Design, il s'agissait d'un stalactite de soie froissée de couleur vive qui n'aurait pas paru déplacé dans une casbah marocaine. Aujourd'hui considéré comme un classique du design en Allemagne, c'est grâce à lui que Wylly a rencontré sa femme et associée Birgit Israel. Ayant reconnu tout le potentiel du luminaire, cette dernière a traqué son créateur et a fini par l'épouser. Jusqu'à récemment, la société et le couple cohabitaient dans ce loft de Shoreditch, mais les affaires l'ont emporté, grignotant peu à peu l'espace privé des tourtereaux. Aujourd'hui, Wylly et Israel ont déménagé et le loft s'est converti en un luxueux bureau.

Peter Wylly & Birgit Israel

The influence of hard-edged 1980s-style minimalism has for a long time dictated that lighting design should be inconspicuous, preferably completely hidden – until the appearance a few years ago of a colourful "wrapped-silk lampshade". Designed by Peter Wylly of Babylon Design, the shade was a stalactite of vivid crumpled silk that wouldn't have looked out of place in a Moroccan kasbah. Considered a design classic today in Germany, it was also responsible for bringing Wylly together with his wife and business partner Birgit Israel after she recognised the design's potential and hunted him down. Until recently, the company and the couple coexisted in this Shoreditch loft, but eventually the business won when the couple realised they valued their privacy at home too much. They moved out and the loft is now the ultimate luxury office.

Der Einfluss des wenig lieblichen Minimalismus der 1980er Jahre gibt seit langem die Direktive vor, dass Licht-Design unauffällig zu sein hat, vorzugsweise überhaupt nicht sichtbar ist – bis vor einigen Jahren ein in leuchtenden Seidenstoffen »eingewickelter« Lampenschirm die Szene betrat. Entworfen hat ihn Peter Wylly von Babylon Design – als organisch wirkenden Stalaktiten, geformt aus zerknüllter, leuchtender Seide, der ebenso gut in eine marokkanische Kasbah gepasst hätte. In Deutschland gilt dieser Entwurf schon jetzt als Klassiker. Außerdem stiftete er eine Ehe, denn er brachte Peter Wylly und seine spätere Frau und Geschäftspartnerin Birgit Israel zusammen. Sie hatte das Potential dieses Entwurfs erkannt und daraufhin versucht, den Designer hinter der Lampe ausfindig zu machen. Bis vor kurzem waren Firma und Ehepaar in diesem Loft in Shoreditch noch eins, doch dann siegte die Firma, denn Peter Wylly und seiner Frau wurde klar, wie wichtig ihnen die häusliche Privatsphäre war. Sie zogen aus und machten aus dem Loft das ultimative Luxus-Büro.

First page: Wylly and Israel in their loft.
Above: On the recessed shelf, which stretches the length of one wall, is Wylly's white ovoid incense burner, designed for the Body Shop.
Facing page: Paul Goldman's "Cherner" chair stands next to a standard lamp with a woven-card shade by Wylly and a corrugated-paper floor lamp by Roland Simmons for Babylon Design.

Première page: Wylly et Israel dans leur loft.
Ci-dessus: Sur l'étagère encastrée qui court tout le long d'un des murs, le brûleur d'encens ovoïde que Wylly a dessiné pour le Body Shop.
Page de droite: La chaise «Cherner» de Paul Goldman est placée à côté d'un lampadaire standard surmonté d'un abat-jour en carton tressé de Wylly et d'un luminaire en papier ondulé de Roland Simmons pour Babylon Design.

Eingangsseite: Peter Wylly und Birgit Israel in ihrem Loft.
Oben: Auf dem eingetieften Sims, der sich über die Länge einer ganzen Wand zieht, steht Peter Wyllys weißer, eiförmiger Räucherstäbchen-Halter, den er für den Body Shop entwarf.
Rechte Seite: Paul Goldmans »Cherner«-Stuhl neben einer Stehleuchte mit Schirm aus gekardeter Wolle von Wylly und einem Bodenlicht aus Wellpappe, das Roland Simmons für Babylon Design entwarf.

Addresses / Adresses / Adressen

ANTIQUES & COLLECTABLES

Bazar
82, Golborne Road, W10
Phone (020) 89 69 62 62

Decorative Living
55, New King's Road, SW6
Phone (020) 77 36 56 23

Nick Haywood
198, Westbourne Grove, W11
Phone (020) 77 27 87 08
Fax (020) 77 27 28 90

Solaris @ Milio Interiors
170, Westbourne Grove, W11
Phone (020) 72 29 81 00
Fax (020) 72 29 83 00
e-mail solaris11@msn.com

ARCHITECTURAL SALVAGE

LASSCo
St Michaels & All Angels
Church, Mark Street, EC2
Phone (020) 77 39 04 48
Fax (020) 77 29 68 53
www.lassco.co.uk

Architectural Salvage Centre
Theobalds Park Road, Enfield,
EN2
Phone (020) 83 67 75 77

AUCTION HOUSES

Christie's
85, Old Brompton Road, SW7
Phone (020) 75 81 76 11
8, King's Street, St. James,
SW1
Phone (020) 78 39 90 60
www.christies.com

Sotheby's
34, New Bond Street, W1
Phone (020) 72 93 50 00
www.sothebys.com

Phillip's
101, New Bond Street, W1
Phone (020) 76 29 66 02
10, Salem Road, W2
Phone (020) 72 29 90 90
www.phillips-auctions.com

Criterion Auctioneers
53–55, Essex Road,
Islington, N1
Phone (020) 73 59 57 07

BOOK SHOPS

RIBA Bookshop
66, Portland Place, W1
Phone (020) 72 51 07 91
www.ribabookshop.com

Zwemmer
80, Charing Cross Road,
Covent Garden, WC2
Phone (020) 72 40 41 57
Fax (020) 72 40 41 86
Zwemmers at The Whitechapel
80, Whitechapel High Street, E1
Phone (020) 72 47 69 24

Magma
8, Earlham Street, WC2
Phone (020) 72 40 84 98

Dillon's
213, Piccadilly, W1
Phone (020) 74 34 96 17

CARPETS & RUGS

Wool Classics
41, Ledbury Road, W11
Phone (020) 77 92 82 77
Fax (020) 77 92 05 81
Chelsea Harbour Design
Centre
Phone (020) 73 49 00 90
Fax (020) 73 40 00 35

The Carpet Library
148, Wandsworth Bridge Road,
SW6
Phone (020) 77 36 36 64

Roger Oates Design Co.Ltd
1, Munro Terrace, off Riley
Street, SW10
Phone (020) 73 51 22 88

DESIGN CENTRES

Oxo Tower
Oxo Tower Wharf,
Bargehouse Street, SE1
Phone (020) 74 01 22 55
Fax (020) 79 28 01 11
Young and innovative design
studios featuring everything
from furniture and lighting to
textiles and ceramics.
www.london-se1.co.uk/
attractions/oxo.html

**Chelsea Harbour Design
Centre**
Chelsea Harbour, SW10
Phone (020) 77 61 86 00
Fax (020) 73 52 78 68
www.chdc.co.uk/
Trade interior design centre
specialising in fabrics, furnish-
ing accessories and furniture.
A wide selection of internat-
ional names including :
Sahco Hesslein, Donghia,
Le Lièvre, Jim Thompson,
Colefax & Fowler, Altfield

DESIGNERS & ARCHITECTS

**Solange Azagury-Partridge,
jewellery and interiors**
171, Westbourne Grove, W11
Phone (020) 77 92 01 97

**Liza Bruce, swimwear and
clothing**
9, Pont Street, SW1
Phone (020) 72 35 84 23
Fax (020) 72 45 97 54
e-mail Lizabruce@aol.com

Nicholas Alvis Vega, furniture
(020) 79 38 15 78

Ozwald Boateng Couture
83, Wimpole Street, W1
Phone (020) 75 63 98 00
Fax (020) 74 87 57 37

VX Design and architecture
Unit 4, 185, Old Brompton
Road, SW5
Phone/Fax (020) 73 70 54 96
e-mail Vx@onetel.net.uk
www.vx.com

Shaun Clarkson ID
Unit 6, 8–13, New Inn Street,
EC2
Phone (020) 77 39 68 65
Fax (020) 77 39 68 64
e-mail
shaun@scid.demon.co.uk
www.shaunclarkson.co.uk

The New RenaisCAnce
14, West Central Street, WC1
Phone (020) 72 40 83 02

Agent Provocateur, lingerie
119, Charterhouse Street, EC1
Phone (020) 72 53 51 23
6, Broadwick Street, W1
Phone (020) 74 39 02 29
16, Pont Street, SW3
Phone (020) 72 35 02 29

Christian de Falbe, interiors
The Glasshouse, 49 A
Goldhawk Road, W12
Phone/Fax (020) 87 43 32 10
e-mail studio@cdef.co.uk

Judy Kleinman Design
Fax (020) 72 21 82 36

Max Inc., interiors
5, Holly Bush Hill, NW3
Phone (020) 73 23 52 50

Rude of London
Sera Hersham-Loftus
Phone (020) 72 86 59 48
www.rudeoflondon.com

**Adjaye and Russell
Architecture & Design**
24, Sunbury Workshops,
Swanfield Street, E2
Phone (020) 77 39 49 69
Fax (020) 77 39 34 84
e-mail
dadjaye@compuserve.com

John Pawson
Unit B
70–78, York Way, N1
Phone (020) 78 37 2929
Fax (020) 78 37 49 49

Reed Creative Services Ltd
151a, Sydney Street, SW3
Phone (020) 75 65 00 66
Fax (020) 75 65 00 67
e-mail
studio@ReedCreative.co.uk

Rolf Sachs Function
101, Farm Lane, SW6
Phone (020) 76 10 07 77
Fax (020) 73 86 93 44
e-mail rolfsachs@aol.com

**Cookie London, children's
clothing**
Phone (020) 72 21 39 64

**Michael Sodeau Partnership,
furniture and product design**
Studio 26
26, Roseberry Avenue, EC1
Phone (020) 78 33 50 20
Fax (020) 78 33 50 21
e-mail info@msp.uk.com

DESIGNER LIVING

Nicole Farhi
16, Fouberts Place, W1
Phone (020) 72 87 87 87
Fax (020) 72 87 23 67

Browns Focus
38–39, South Molton Street
Phone (020) 76 29 06 66

FABRIC and WALL PAPER

Colefax & Fowler
19/23, Grosvenor Hill, W1
Phone (020) 74 93 22 31
Fax (020) 74 95 31 23
www.iida.co.uk/cf.html

V V Rouleaux
54, Sloane Square, Cliveden
Place, SW1
Phone (020) 77 30 31 25
trimmings and tassels etc.

FLOORING and WALLS,
including TILES, STONE
LEATHER & RUBBER

Paris Ceramics Ltd
583, King's Road, SW6
Phone (020) 73 71 77 78
www.parisceramics.com

Stone Age Ltd
19, Filmer Road, SW6
Phone (020) 73 85 79 54

Perucchetti Associates
RMC House
15, Townmead Road, SW6
Phone (020) 73 71 71 06
polished plaster

Dalsouple Direct Ltd.
Phone for trade enquiries
(01984) 66 72 33
Phone for retail
(01984) 66 75 51
e-mail info@dalsouple.com
www.dalsouple.com

Hardwood Flooring Co Ltd
146, West End Lane, NW6
Phone (020) 73 28 84 81
Fax (020) 76 25 59 51
www.hardwood-
flooring.uk.com

Mosaik Ltd
10, Kensington Square, W8
Phone (020) 77 95 62 53

Bill Amberg
10, Chepstow Road W2
Phone (020) 77 27 35 60
leather floors

FURNITURE – 20th CENTURY

twentyonetwentyone
274, Upper Street, N1
Phone (020) 72 88 19 96

Tom Tom
42, New Compton Street, WC2
Phone/Fax (020) 72 40 79 09
e-mail
sales@tomtomshop.co.uk
www.tomtomshop.co.uk

Century Design
68, Marylebone High Street, W1
Phone (020) 74 87 51 00

**FURNITURE –
CONTEMPORARY AND
CLASS C**

David Gill
3, Loughborough Street, SE11
Phone (020) 77 93 11 00
60, Fulham Road, SW3
Phone (020) 75 89 59 46

Succession
179, Westbourne Grove, W11
Phone (020) 77 27 05 80

SCP
135-139, Curtain Road, EC2
Phone (020) 77 39 18 69
Fax (020) 77 29 42 24
www.scp.co.uk

Spencer Fung Architects
3, Pinemews, NW10
Phone (020) 89 60 98 83
Fax (020) 89 60 93 39
sfarch@compuserve.com

Eurolounge Tom Dixon
28, All Saints Road, W11
Phone (020) 77 92 54 99
Fax (020) 77 92 54 88
e-mail:
info@eurolounge.co.uk
www.eurolounge.co.uk

Vitra Ltd
30, Clerkenwell Road, EC1
Phone (020) 76 08 62 00
Fax (020) 76 08 62 01
e-mail info_uk@vitra.com
www.vitra.com

Ligne Roset Chiswick
418-422, Chiswick High Road,
W4
Phone (020) 89 95 77 22
Fax (020) 89 95 77 33
Ligne Roset West End
23-25, Mortimer Street, W1
Phone (020) 73 23 12 48
Fax (020) 73 23 12 47
http://www.ligne-roset-
london.co.uk

GALLERIES

Anthony d'Offay
9, 23, 24, Derring Street, W1
Phone (020) 74 99 41 00
Fax (020) 74 93 44 43
doffay.com/page9.htm

Saatchi
98a, Boundary Road, NW8
Phone (020) 76 24 82 99

White Cube
44, Duke Street, St James, SW1
Phone (020) 79 30 53 73
Fax (020) 79 30 99 73
e-mail
enquiries@whitecube.com
www.whitecube.com

Sadie Coles HQ
35, Heddon Street, W1
Phone (020) 74 34 22 27

KITCHEN EQUIPMENT

Summerill & Bishop Ltd
100, Portland Road, W11
Phone (020) 72 21 45 66

LIFESTYLE SHOPS

The Cross
141, Portland Road, W11
Phone (020) 77 27 67 60

Mission
45, Hereford Road, W2
Phone (020) 72 29 22 92
Fax (020) 72 29 98 91

Egg
36, Kinnerton Street, SW1
Phone (020) 72 35 93 15

Space
214, Westbourne Grove, W11
Phone (020) 72 29 65 33

Bowles & Linares
32, Hereford Road, W2
Phone (020) 72 29 98 86

Carden Cunetti
83, Westbourne Park Road, W2
Phone (020) 72 29 85 59
Fax (020) 72 29 87 99
www.carden-cunetti.com

David Champion Ltd
199, Westbourne Grove, W11
Phone (020) 77 27 60 16

Pure Living
1-3, Leonard Street, EC2
Phone (020) 72 50 1116
Fax (020) 72 50 0616
e-mail
mail@puredesignuk.com

Alma Home
12–14, Greatorex Street, E1
Phone (020) 73 77 07 62

LIGHTING

Babylon
301, Fulham Road, SW10
Phone (020) 73 76 7255

McCloud Lighting Ltd
269, Wandsworth Bridge
Road, SW6
Phone (020) 73 71 71 51
www.mccloud.co.uk

The Lighting Store
62–64, Baker Street, W1
Phone (020) 74 87 50 70

MARKETS

Portobello
Portobello Road, W10
Friday to Sunday

Camden
Chalk Farm Road, Camden
High Street, NW1
Saturday and Sunday

Bermondsey
Bermondsey Square, SE1
Friday

Brick Lane
Brick Lane, Cygnet Street,
Sclater St, E1
Sunday

Alfies Antique Market
13–25, Church Street, NW8
Phone (020) 77 23 60 66

PAINTS & PIGMENTS

Paint Library
5, Elystan Street, SW3
Phone (020) 78 23 77 55

Papers & Paints Ltd
4, Park Walk, Chelsea, SW10
Phone (020) 73 52 86 26

L Cornelissen & Son Ltd
105, Great Russell Street, WC1
Phone (020) 76 36 10 45

SPECIALIST SHOPS

Wild at Heart
49a, Ledbury Road, W11
Phone (020) 77 27 30 95
Florist

Dyala Salam
174a, Kensington Church
Street, W8
Phone (020) 72 29 40 45
Turkish textiles and glass

Paul Reeves
32b, Kensington Church
Street, W8
Phone (020) 79 37 15 94
Arts & Crafts and Mackintosh
furniture

Get Stuffed
105, Essex Road, N1
Phone (020) 72 26 13 64
Fax (020) 73 59 82 53
stuffed animals

Mac London
142, Clerkenwell Road, EC1
Phone (020) 77 13 12 34
www.mac-london.com
eccentricities and classic furniture

**Gallery of Antique Costume &
Textiles**
2, Church Street, Marylebone,
NW8
Phone/Fax (020) 77 23 99 81
www.gact.co.uk

Snap Dragon
247, Fulham Road, SW3
Phone (020) 73 76 88 89
Oriental